·GRAPHIC·
DESIGN
FOR
EVERYONE

CONSULTANT EDITOR

CATH CALDWELL

·GRAPHIC·
DESIGN
FOR
EVERYONE

Senior Editor	Rona Skene
Senior Art Editor	Alison Gardner
Editors	Philippa Dawson, Alice Horne
Designers	Steve Marsden, Hannah Moore, Collette Sadler, Sophie State
Illustrator	Steve Marsden
Picture Researcher	Rituraj Singh
Producer, Pre-Production	David Almond
Producer	Luca Bazzoli
Senior Jacket Creative	Saffron Stocker
Jacket Co-ordinator	Lucy Philpott
Creative Technical Support	Sonia Charbonnier
Managing Editor	Dawn Henderson
Managing Art Editor	Marianne Markham
Art Director	Maxine Pedliham
Publishing Director	Mary-Clare Jerram

First published in Great Britain in 2019
by Dorling Kindersley Limited, 80 Strand, London, WC2R 0RL

Copyright © 2019 Dorling Kindersley Limited
A Penguin Random House Company
10 9 8 7 6 5 4 3 2 1
001–310528–July/2019

A CIP catalogue record for this book is available
from the British Library.
ISBN: 978-0-2413-4381-4

Printed and bound in China

All images © Dorling Kindersley Limited
For further information see: www.dkimages.com

A WORLD OF IDEAS:
SEE ALL THERE IS TO KNOW

www.dk.com

CONSULTANT AND AUTHORS

CONSULTANT EDITOR

Cath Caldwell is senior lecturer at Central Saint Martins, the world-leading design college at University of the Arts London, where she teaches graphic communication design and fashion journalism as well as lecturing in Europe. She strives to make design accessible to all and is researching equality and inclusion in the arts education sector. Formerly design director at *ELLE UK*, Cath has also worked for the *Observer*, the *Guardian*, and Condé Nast in New York. This is her third book on graphic design.

THE AUTHORS

Johnny Belknap is a native New Yorker who cut his design teeth on the iconic *Village Voice* newspaper in the 1970s. He moved on to art director roles at *7 Days* magazine, *The American Lawyer*, and the *New York Times*. In the UK, Johnny has been art director at the *Sunday Telegraph Magazine*, *Blueprint*, the *Daily Express*, and the *Jewish Chronicle*. He also found time to run his own design studio, which relaunched publications around the world – from Dublin to São Paulo.

Johnny wrote the Image section in the chapter entitled *Building Blocks*.

Jamie Sanchez Hearn is a graphic designer and lecturer, specializing in Typography, Branding, and Editorial Design. With 10 years of industry experience, he has worked for several international design agencies, before forming his own design studio collaborating with clients in Spain, Sweden, and the UK. Jamie currently teaches on a variety of undergraduate and short courses at Central Saint Martins and is a fellow of the UK's Higher Education Academy.

Jamie wrote the Type and Colour sections in the chapter entitled *Building Blocks*.

Emily Wood is a graphic designer and lecturer. Before co-founding REG Design in 2003, she worked for leading design studios Pentagram, Johnson Banks, and Bloom. She has worked with a range of cultural organizations, including London's V&A Museum, the Crafts Council, and Amnesty International. Emily's research is focused on sustainability through education and design, and has included collaborations with Save The Children.

Emily wrote the chapter entitled *Putting It Together*.

Julia Woollams is a graphic designer, branding consultant, and part-time lecturer. After honing her talent at world-renowned agency Johnson Banks, she co-founded creative consultancy 31% Wool. Julia specializes in cultural and not-for-profit sectors and has worked with many organizations in the past 20 years, including London's V&A Museum, King's College London, La Villette, the Science Museum, the Sendai Observatory, and the University of Cambridge.

Julia wrote the chapter entitled *Understanding Your Brand*.

CONTENTS

PUTTING IT TOGETHER

PRODUCING YOUR DESIGNS

FOREWORD

We are living in an exhilarating time for design, with a range of digital tools never before available to the graphic designer. All over the world, communities and individuals can make their own designs to benefit their purpose, product, or cause. No longer the exclusive domain of "professionals", graphic design today is accessible to all.

I would have loved that idea when I was younger. As a child I hand-drew posters for community fêtes and tried to draw my own typefaces. I won a prize for a school anti-litter campaign. My dad was a type compositor and instilled in me a lasting respect for type. I designed my first logo for my uncle's refrigeration repair company – my earliest attempt at branding design. In those pre-internet days, design was for the specialist, so I learned traditional hand-artwork skills at art college and gained printing knowledge on press in the magazine industry. That's all ancient history. Now my daughter uses her phone to make videos, to create fonts, to set up a website and to delight her Instagram followers. It's so accessible and so much more fun!

It is important that the tried and trusted principles of design are not put aside, however. Even in a digital age, my students still want to know what makes good design "work". No matter what medium you are working in, the goal of graphic design remains the same – to use type, images, space, shapes, and colour so that you can communicate visually in the most effective way with your audience.

My creative work is all about demystifying graphic design and helping non-professionals to discover how empowering and creative design can be. To achieve this, I draw on my experiences as a design director in New York, as a teacher of graphic design in London, and as a partner running a design studio. My ambition for this project was to provide an easy-to-follow, one-stop design resource for the total beginner, the self-taught and the intermediate designer alike. What I love most about the book we've produced is that it doesn't just tell you how it's done, it shows you – with specially commissioned, beautifully clear graphics that illustrate the most important things you need to know. Step by step, we take you through the whole design process – from researching your target audience and building a brand to publishing your work in print or online.

Once you've got to grips with branding, we introduce the building blocks you're going to need, explaining exactly how to use type and image within both digital and printed layouts. Then we show you how to put it all together, including a primer in the hierarchy and composition used in design. We've also gathered some resources and advice on producing and publishing your designs. Throughout the book, you'll find practical projects that show you how to design leaflets, a web page, an e-shop, product labels, and much more. And for inspiration, we showcase the best and most iconic graphic design from around the world, past and present.

Whether you already have some experience or you're a complete beginner, I hope you will feel inspired to create your own designs and release your hidden talents. Visual skill begins with a great idea and good basic strategy. When you are more practised, you can learn to trust your "good eye" for layout, photography, or colour and use this book as a resource to develop your skills further.

I'm proud of this book, and of the writers who have so willingly shared with you their expertise and enthusiasm for making graphic design. We hope it helps you to succeed in your enterprises, businesses, charities, and community groups. Enjoy the journey! You have no reason to doubt yourself – this is the best time to be a designer. Because right now, graphic design really is for everyone.

Cath Caldwell

SENIOR LECTURER, CENTRAL SAINT MARTINS
AT UNIVERSITY OF THE ARTS LONDON

UNDERSTANDING YOUR BRAND }

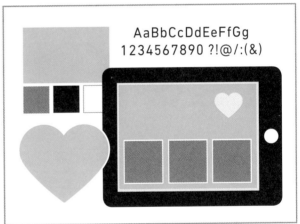

YOU AND YOUR
AUDIENCE }

The first step in the design process is to think about your project objectives, your competitors, and what makes you different. Your aim is to consolidate your brand message and think strategically about your audience. The decisions you make at this stage are crucial to giving you confidence in the graphic design approach you take. For every hour you spend now in planning, you will save many more hours when you start designing. Time to get started...

DEFINE YOUR PROJECT AIMS

MAKE IT PERSONAL

As you go through this exercise, bear in mind that you, your project, and your brand are inextricably linked. Your project is probably something that's close to your heart, so your own personal aims and values will likely overlap with those of your project. The more the project's goals chime with your own, the more authentic your communications will be – and authenticity is what builds the audience's trust in your project.

WHAT'S THE MAIN AIM?
WHAT ELSE COULD YOU ACHIEVE?

The first step is to decide what you consider to be the most important outcome of your project. It might be obvious, but if you find it hard to pin down, try posing more specific questions and see what you come up with. Do you want to raise money for a specific purpose? Attract supporters? Find a new or different customer base for your products?

There are no right or wrong answers, and you are likely to end up with more than one project aim. Your ambitions may differ depending on whether you are starting something new, or thinking about extending a concern that already exists. To show how you might go about defining your aims, this example is for a charity fundraising event. You could apply the same technique for any project or venture.

The starting point for any design project is to define the outcome you want. A clear set of aims or objectives will enable you to make the design decisions that will ensure you achieve the best results.

CHARITY FUNDRAISER EVENT: **AIMS**

Writing down and ranking your aims, then forming a project brief are good ways to keep your project on track. The main aim of the event is to raise money on the day for the good cause, but there are other, more long-term objectives to bear in mind when designing publicity and event-day materials.

1 RAISE FUNDS THROUGH SPONSORSHIP

Set your project aims in order of importance

2 RAISE AWARENESS OF THE CAUSE

3 RECRUIT PARTICIPANTS

If aims have equal importance, place them on the same level

4 RECRUIT VOLUNTEERS FOR THE EVENT

5 STAND OUT FROM OTHER FUNDRAISERS

6 CONNECT WITH POTENTIAL SUPPORTERS

FUNDRAISER: **BRIEF**

Use the aims to form the basis of a short brief to refer to as you work on the project. A brief is especially useful if you are planning to enlist the help of others – it helps them understand what you are hoping to achieve.

Fundraising event

BRIEF

The main aim has been established: to raise funds on the day. The secondary aims are to raise awareness of our cause, and to attract potential helpers and donors. The brief, therefore, is to further those aims by creating a consistent and unique design approach to promoting the event both online and in print. This will ensure that potential event volunteers, participants, and donors are kept as well informed as possible.

ANALYSE YOUR STYLE – AND YOUR COMPETITORS'

RESEARCH AND ANALYSE

Whether your project is new, or you are refreshing or extending it, auditing your verbal and visual style – how you talk and how you look – is essential, so that you can decide how to go forward.

It's also useful to examine other projects to help you think about how to stand out from them, and where to place yourself in the market. The process of analysing others is known as a peer or competitor audit.

YOU

TASK 1

AUDIT YOURSELF

If you are starting from scratch, you may have little or nothing to audit yet. If so, go on to task 2. If your project is already up and running, run through these steps to get an overview of your current situation.

EVALUATE YOUR COMMUNICATIONS

Look at every medium in which you promote yourself. This could include:

- website
- blog
- social media pages
- business cards
- flyers
- brochures
- adverts
- shop signage
- staff clothing

Successful design enables you to stand out, as well as appeal specifically to a target audience. Taking stock of your current or planned style of communication and comparing it to others in your area will help you find a design approach that's both individual and effective.

WHAT TO CONSIDER:

Verbal style:
- Project/brand name
- Do you have a strapline?
- How you describe yourself (your brand story)
- Your tone of voice – are your words chatty, formal, neutral, or something else?

Visual style:
- Your current logo
- The project's fonts
- The project's colour palette
- Imagery – photographs and illustrations
- The way these visual elements are combined (layout)

NOW ASK YOURSELF...

Are elements consistent wherever you promote yourself?

Consistency is crucial as it helps your audience remember your brand.

Objectively, how do you rate your communications?

- Do you speak too formally?
- Does your colour palette look dated?
- What needs to change?
- If you're struggling to see your project in an impartial way, try asking friends. Once you have completed the audit, you'll be well placed to decide what, if anything, needs to change.

OTHERS

TASK 2

EVALUATE PEERS AND COMPETITORS

If you had an existing project to analyse, the second task is to look at others in your field.

Start by listing all the other projects you know of that are similar to yours. Let's say you are opening a coffee shop: you'll need to find out which other cafés are already trading locally. A simple internet search will help with your list if you're not sure who your competitors are. Don't worry if you don't find every competitor out there – you just need to get a feel for how similar projects are communicating. It's best to find out now, for example, that your logo idea is already out there and being used in a similar project.

Repeat the steps in task 1 to analyse each competitor, and note your observations on how they promote themselves verbally and visually.

MAP THE MARKET AND PLOT YOUR POSITION

WHO'S WHO IN YOUR SECTOR

Look back at your audit and think about the characteristics of your competitors and peers. Choose the two features that you think are most important – for instance how expensive, and how traditional/modern they are – and write a brief assessment of each competitor. This example follows a coffee shop looking to relaunch in a high street with some keen competition.

MAPPING THE HIGH STREET COFFEE SHOPS

Draw two intersecting lines, or axes. In this example, the horizontal axis runs from "Traditional" to "Modern" and the vertical axis from "Budget" to "Luxury". This creates four segments in which to place your competitors, according to your assessments of their style. For an existing project, place yourself where you think you currently are. Are you happy there? Should you look for a new place in the sector? For a new project, look at the gaps and place yourself where you want to be.

THE COMPETITORS

COFFEE TO GO
Verbal: mix of formal and conversational language
Visual: looks amateurish, not consistent across different media
Price: One of the cheapest

COFFEE ORGANICS
Verbal: friendly, inclusive, pro-green stance
Visual: earthy, natural
Price: mid-range

TRADITIONAL

POSH BEANS
Verbal: uses very descriptive and formal language
Visual: looks sophisticated, but conservative
Price: the most expensive

COFFEE WITH A KICK
Verbal: uses friendly, urban, chatty language
Visual: looks unusual, professional, and consistent
Price: Upper end of the scale

CAFÉ CULTURE
Verbal: uses straightforward, street language
Visual: looks fun, hip, and youthful
Price: Lower end of the scale

COOL CAFÉ
Verbal: communication style varies
Visual: minimal styling and use of colour is haphazard
Price: the cheapest

Once you have audited yourself and your competitors, you can use the information to plot where you all currently sit in the sector. This is a good way to spot any gaps in the market that your project could fill. This technique is sometimes known as market mapping.

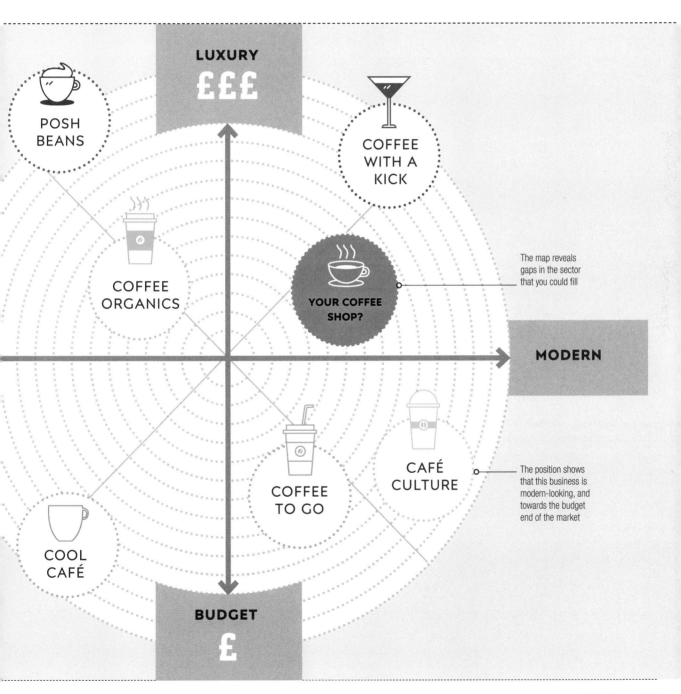

LUXURY
£££

POSH
BEANS

COFFEE
WITH A
KICK

COFFEE
ORGANICS

YOUR COFFEE
SHOP?

The map reveals
gaps in the sector
that you could fill

MODERN

CAFÉ
CULTURE

The position shows
that this business is
modern-looking, and
towards the budget
end of the market

COFFEE
TO GO

COOL
CAFÉ

BUDGET
£

DEFINE WHAT YOUR PROJECT STANDS FOR

INTERVIEW YOURSELF

Defining what your project stands for is essential in helping you to start to formulate your brand. A good way to start the process is to interview yourself. Ask yourself this set of questions to help you to find the essence of your project. Some questions overlap to get you to think about your project from slightly different angles. The questions are a starting point – you can tweak them or add more to address the specifics of your project. If you're working with colleagues, ask them to do the interview, too. A range of views can help you refine or even re-evaluate what your project stands for.

THE INTERVIEW
Questions you might ask yourself

WHEN YOU ANSWER
Things to consider in your replies

1   WHAT DOES MY PROJECT DO?

How would you sum the project up to someone you don't know? Be as concise as you can.

2   HOW DOES MY PROJECT DO IT?

How does the project operate on a day-to-day basis?

3   WHAT IS MY PROJECT'S MAIN PURPOSE?

Reminding yourself of your project's reason for being will drive you forward. See page 14 for how to clarify your project's aims.

4   WHO IS MY PROJECT FOR?

This is all about your audience – who are you targeting? What sort of customer or client do you think you'll attract?

5   WHY IS MY PROJECT HERE?

Why did you want to start this project? If you have lots of reasons, try to pinpoint your main motivation.

Before starting on design, you need to lay the foundations of a brand. There has to be a good reason for you to pick those colours, choose those fonts, or craft your logo in that way. Deciding what makes your project unique and worthwhile will be crucial when you come to make those choices.

6　**HOW** WOULD I DESCRIBE MY PROJECT'S PERSONALITY?

Thinking of your project as a person will help you find and communicate with the right audience. Is it loud or quiet? Reserved or friendly? Assertive or modest?

7　**WHAT** TONE OF VOICE DOES MY PROJECT HAVE?

Think about your intended audience. How would your project speak, if it could? Would it be chatty or formal? Authoritative or confiding? Serious or light-hearted?

8　**WHAT** DO I (AND MY PROJECT) VALUE MOST?

What is the single most important thing to you personally about this project? It could be profit, making a difference, being the best in your field, or something else entirely.

9　**WHAT** MAKES MY PROJECT DIFFERENT?

Consider the unique qualities your project has, which could benefit your audience. This is key, as your uniqueness sets you apart from the competition.

10　**WHICH** BRANDS DO I ADMIRE, AND WHY?

Learn from brands you like. Are the staff always friendly? Do they post great content on social media? Do they make you feel part of a community? The brand doesn't need to be in your sector.

ANALYSIS

These answers will inform your choices as you develop your brand further. You could turn your analysis into a findings report or make a list of simple key messages to be used as the basis for brainstorming your brand message (*see* overleaf), and for the "brand story" element of your verbal brand (*see* page 32, Draft your verbal brand).

BRAINSTORM YOUR BRAND MESSAGE

CREATE A MIND MAP

These simple steps will help you build a mind map for your project.

① PUT YOURSELF AT THE CENTRE

Put the name of your project prominently in the centre of a large sheet of paper or document.

② DECIDE ON CATEGORIES

Decide on the questions you will address, and space them around your project name. You can always add more questions later.

③ CONNECT TO THE CENTRE

Draw lines to connect your questions to your project. You can use colours or icons to distinguish the question.

④ ADD YOUR ANSWERS

Write your thoughts and answers around each question. Vary the size of answers to indicate their relative importance.

⑤ MAKE CONNECTIONS

Draw lines to connect each answer to its question.

⑥ PICK OUT KEY INFORMATION

Emphasize any key words or phrases within your answers in bold or with a coloured highlighter.

⑦ PUT THE MAP ON SHOW

Print your mind map, then pin it up where it is easy to view. Leave it for a while and do something else.

⑧ REVIEW AND REVISE

Revisit the map over the next few days. With fresh eyes, you'll be better able to judge if you need to change or add anything.

EXAMPLE: COMMUNITY WEBSITE

This is how a mind map might look for a website set up to promote a neighbourhood and to inform and connect people who live, work, and socialize there.

LOCAL RESIDENTS

PEOPLE RUNNING **LOCAL EVENTS**

LOCAL COUNCIL

TOURISTS

WHO ARE WE HERE FOR?

YOUNG PROFESSIONAL (20–40YR OLDS)

PEOPLE WHO **WORK** HERE

PHOTOGRAPH EVENTS AND PLACES

MANAGE SOCIAL MEDIA CONTENT

RESEARCH LOCAL EVENTS

WHAT DO WE DO AND HOW?

SUPPORT **LOCAL PROJECTS**

DESIGN BLOG CONTENT

CREATE SOCIAL MEDIA CONTENT

PROMOTE THE LOCAL AREA

WRITE ABOUT EVENTS AND PLACES

Your self-interview has yielded a wealth of thoughts and information – the next step is to organize and visualize that data. A mind map (also known as a spider diagram) gives a great overview of a project – its branching format is much easier for our brains to understand than a linear one.

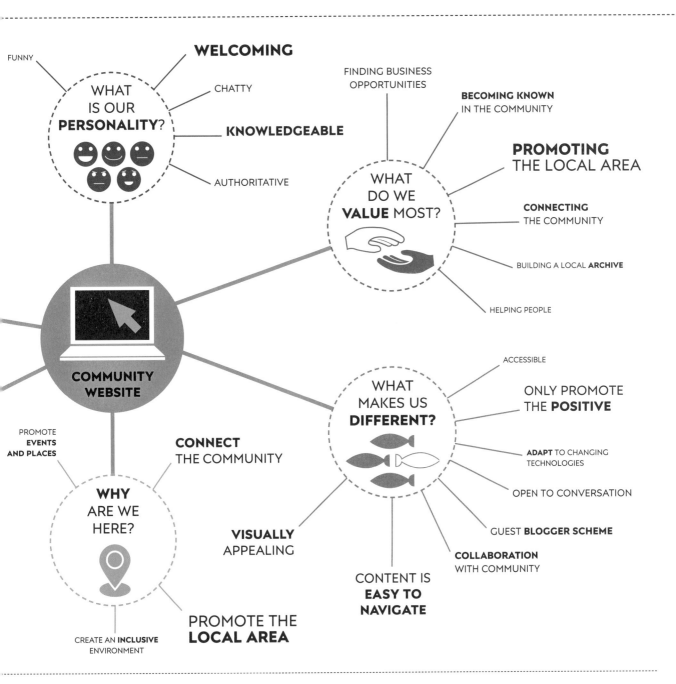

FUNNY

WELCOMING

CHATTY

WHAT
IS OUR
PERSONALITY?

KNOWLEDGEABLE

AUTHORITATIVE

FINDING BUSINESS
OPPORTUNITIES

BECOMING KNOWN
IN THE COMMUNITY

PROMOTING
THE LOCAL AREA

WHAT
DO WE
VALUE MOST?

CONNECTING
THE COMMUNITY

BUILDING A LOCAL **ARCHIVE**

HELPING PEOPLE

**COMMUNITY
WEBSITE**

ACCESSIBLE

WHAT
MAKES US
DIFFERENT?

ONLY PROMOTE
THE **POSITIVE**

ADAPT TO CHANGING
TECHNOLOGIES

OPEN TO CONVERSATION

GUEST **BLOGGER SCHEME**

COLLABORATION
WITH COMMUNITY

PROMOTE
**EVENTS
AND PLACES**

CONNECT
THE COMMUNITY

WHY
ARE WE
HERE?

VISUALLY
APPEALING

CONTENT IS
**EASY TO
NAVIGATE**

CREATE AN **INCLUSIVE**
ENVIRONMENT

PROMOTE THE
LOCAL AREA

RESEARCH YOUR AUDIENCE

TYPES OF AUDIENCE RESEARCH

To find out which types of people are most likely to become your customers or use your service, you need to research the habits of the various groups you might attract. There are two main methods of researching current and potential audiences. Research that you conduct yourself or commission specifically for your project is known as primary research. Gathering and analysing information from existing data and studies is known as secondary research.

QUANTITY VS. QUALITY

Primary and secondary research can be conducted in two main ways, depending on the kind of information you want to gather.

QUANTITATIVE RESEARCH

This research is all about the numbers, telling you, for instance, how many people do something, and how often. Information is gathered through surveys or analytical tools such as Google.

QUALITATIVE RESEARCH

Qualitative researchers record people's thoughts and opinions, rather than hard data. Research is conducted via one-to-one interviews and group discussions (often known as focus groups).

METHOD 1
PRIMARY RESEARCH

Also known as field research, primary research could take the form of interviews, focus groups, surveys, or data you've already directly collected from your project.

PROS:

- You'll get a focused result, as people will be answering your questions, specially formulated for your project.
- If you're carrying out the research yourself, it's low-cost or free.

CONS:

- You can only survey a limited number of users.
- If you commission someone to carry out the research, it can be costly.
- Your research may be too narrow if you don't ask the right range of questions.
- Finding participants can be time-consuming.

CREATING A SURVEY

The aim of a survey is to find out more about who you need to focus on when writing and designing your communications. When creating your survey, keep it as short as you can, while still being useful – people will be much more likely to spare you five minutes than half an hour!

Carry the survey out on different days and times (or in a variety of locations if applicable). This ensures a wider range of people responding. The example shown opposite is a survey by a group campaigning to save a local park from closure. The aim is to find out more about the park's current users, so the campaign can target them.

Finding the right audience is vital to the success of any project – and knowing exactly who you are communicating with will inform all the design decisions you take. If you can, aim to carry out your own research as well as using existing research undertaken by others. Here's how to do it.

EXAMPLE: PARK USERS' SURVEY

1. How old are you?
- ☐ Under 18
- ☐ 18–30
- ☐ 31–45
- ☐ 46–59
- ☐ 60+

2. What is your gender?
- ☐ Female
- ☐ Male
- ☐ Rather not say

3. What is your work status?
- ☐ Not in paid employment
- ☐ Employed part-time
- ☐ Employed full-time
- ☐ Job-seeking
- ☐ Retired

4. Where do you live in relation to the park?
- ☐ Within 1 mile
- ☐ Within 3 miles
- ☐ Within 10 miles
- ☐ Visiting from further away

5. How often do you visit the park?
- ☐ Every day
- ☐ 2–6 times a week
- ☐ Once a week
- ☐ Once a month
- ☐ Twice a year
- ☐ Less than twice a year

6. What do you enjoy most about the park?
- ☐ Nature and wildlife
- ☐ Sport
- ☐ Playground
- ☐ Café
- ☐ Dog-walking
- ☐ Meeting friends

7. Do you regularly care for children?
- ☐ Yes
- ☐ No

8. Where do you get most of your news?
- ☐ TV
- ☐ Newspaper
- ☐ Radio
- ☐ Social media
- ☐ Word of mouth

9. Which social media channels do you use most?
Write in as many as apply

METHOD 2
SECONDARY RESEARCH

Sources of secondary research could include existing reports and studies, data you've found on the internet, or articles from newspapers, magazines, or journals.

PROS:
- You can find lots of secondary research for free.
- You'll access information you wouldn't have the time or budget to gather yourself.
- You can access a large amount of data.

CONS:
- Information might be too general, as it's not answering your specific questions.
- Hunting through data for relevant information can be time-consuming.
- The research isn't unique to you – others can access and use it too.

RESEARCHING SECONDARY SOURCES

A good start is to find official data on the population and groups (demographics) in your area – this information is usually free. In the UK, the Office for National Statistics is a good general source. You could also search, online or at a library, for reports and data that relate specifically to your area of interest. Sources could include official regulators or commercial market research companies.

VISUALIZE YOUR RESEARCH INFORMATION

TURNING DATA INTO A GRAPH

Visualizing information and data as graphs and charts is a handy skill for designers. Here's how to turn survey data into graphs that are easy to analyse.

① COUNT THE RESPONSES

Once you have canvassed enough people, add up the individual responses to each question.

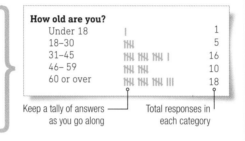

How old are you?

Under 18	I	1
18–30	|||||	5
31–45	||||| ||||| ||||| I	16
46–59	||||| |||||	10
60 or over	||||| ||||| ||||| III	18

Keep a tally of answers as you go along   Total responses in each category

② INPUT THE DATA

The easiest way to create a chart or graph is to input your data to a computer-based spreadsheet tool.

③ DECIDE ON A VISUAL STYLE

The spreadsheet tool will offer a range of ways to illustrate the data you have inputted. In the example on the facing page, bars of different lengths make it easy to identify the most popular responses. Create a graph or chart for each question.

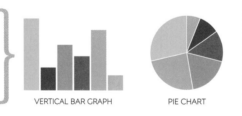

VERTICAL BAR GRAPH   PIE CHART

④ COLOUR-CODE THE RESULTS

Use colour to distinguish the different responses to questions. Use the same colour code in every graph, so that you can easily pick out the most – and least – popular answers.

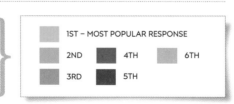

1ST – MOST POPULAR RESPONSE		
2ND	4TH	6TH
3RD	5TH	

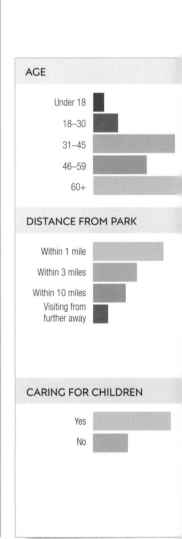

AGE

- Under 18
- 18–30
- 31–45
- 46–59
- 60+

DISTANCE FROM PARK

- Within 1 mile
- Within 3 miles
- Within 10 miles
- Visiting from further away

CARING FOR CHILDREN

- Yes
- No

Turning your data into visuals in the form of graphs or charts is a helpful way for you to analyse the information you've collected. Data is much easier to understand in a visual format, and you'll be able to pick out patterns and trends that will feed into all your design and marketing decisions.

EXAMPLE: SAVE A LOCAL PARK

The data collected from the survey on the previous page has been visualized as a series of horizontal graphs. Viewed together, they allow you to form an overview of the research.

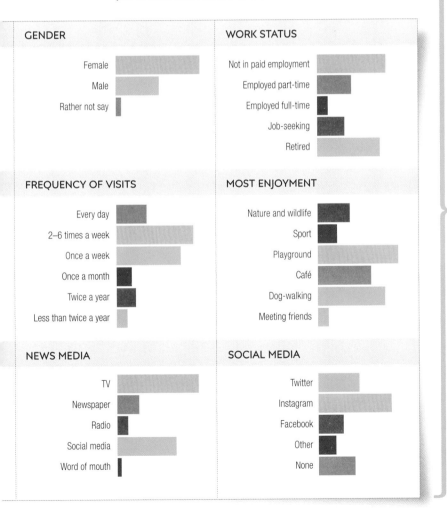

GENDER
- Female
- Male
- Rather not say

WORK STATUS
- Not in paid employment
- Employed part-time
- Employed full-time
- Job-seeking
- Retired

FREQUENCY OF VISITS
- Every day
- 2–6 times a week
- Once a week
- Once a month
- Twice a year
- Less than twice a year

MOST ENJOYMENT
- Nature and wildlife
- Sport
- Playground
- Café
- Dog-walking
- Meeting friends

NEWS MEDIA
- TV
- Newspaper
- Radio
- Social media
- Word of mouth

SOCIAL MEDIA
- Twitter
- Instagram
- Facebook
- Other
- None

ANALYSIS

The data shows who uses and values the park most – these are the people the campaign should target. Two main audiences emerge:
- Younger carers of children, mostly female
- Retired people caring for grandchildren, or dog-walking – again, mostly female

With your target audience identified, you can now start to build a campaign. Your design and communication style, and where and how you publicize the campaign, can be tailored to reach these specific groups.

YOU AND YOUR
BRAND }

Now you have worked on strategy, you can create your own brand and visualize the parts that make up the whole. First, decide where to position yourself. However small your startup, take time now to imagine ways you might grow in the future. Follow the simple steps to making a brand plan and move forward with confidence, building your brand assets as you go. Enjoy the decision-making process – these steps will be invaluable when you get down to creating your designs.

THE MAKEUP OF A BRAND

THE IMPORTANCE OF BRANDING

In design and marketing terms, a brand is a set of characteristics that helps an audience differentiate a business, product, service, or project from its competitors. The term itself is derived from the farming practice of marking livestock with a symbol to denote ownership – similarly, a designer's aim is to "imprint" a certain brand on the psyche of its audience.

Usually, words and images form the basis of this set of characteristics, but a brand can also include other elements, such as sounds or even smells (think of a memorable advertising jingle or the aroma from a favourite bakery shop).

It's a common assumption that branding is something only big companies need to think about, but it can be applied to the smallest, non-commercial venture, helping to achieve consistency and clarity. The benefits of branding are cumulative, too: as your brand becomes more recognizable, you don't have to do as much work, or spend as much money, to get noticed.

THREE ELEMENTS

A brand comprises three distinct components: verbal, visual, and emotional. When successful, the different elements combine to form a cohesive whole, capable of seeping into an audience's psyche and generating a powerful emotional response.

ELEMENT 1
VERBAL BRAND

How you talk about your project in communications is the foundation of your brand, and the starting point for design work (*see* page 33: Draft your verbal brand).

ELEMENT 2
VISUAL BRAND

This is how you visually present yourself. Elements such as colour, typefaces, imagery, and graphics are the building blocks of your visual brand. These are combined to create your logo and visual communications (*see* Chapter 2: Building blocks).

ELEMENT 3
BRAND EMOTIONS

All brands evoke an emotional reaction. Think about a favourite shop, for instance. How do you feel about it? Do you think it's friendly, stylish, or reassuringly reliable? If a brand talks and looks one way but acts in another it won't feel authentic, so won't be trusted by its audience.

Research into your project, message, and audience provides the information that forms the basis of your brand. Branding isn't just for promoting businesses. All projects with an audience should be consistent in the way they look and sound to maximize their reach and effect.

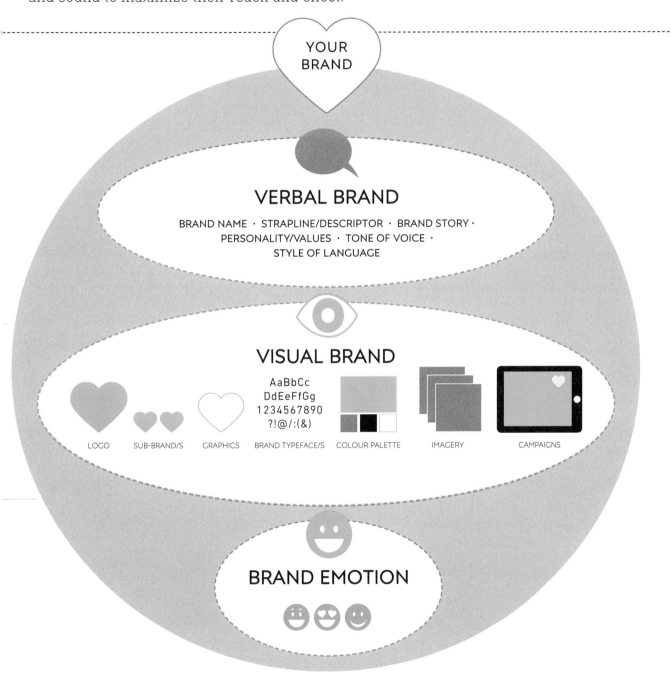

YOUR BRAND

VERBAL BRAND

BRAND NAME · STRAPLINE/DESCRIPTOR · BRAND STORY · PERSONALITY/VALUES · TONE OF VOICE · STYLE OF LANGUAGE

VISUAL BRAND

AaBbCc
DdEeFfGg
1234567890
?!@/:(&)

LOGO   SUB-BRAND/S   GRAPHICS   BRAND TYPEFACE/S   COLOUR PALETTE   IMAGERY   CAMPAIGNS

BRAND EMOTION

DRAFT YOUR VERBAL BRAND

MAKEUP OF A VERBAL BRAND

A verbal brand is made up of different elements, shown here as segments of a whole. To draft a verbal brand, take each element in turn and set down your thoughts. If you have carried out the research and brainstorming tasks described in this chapter, you will already have a lot to work with. This exercise pulls together all that you have learned – then you can hone the wording until you have a verbal brand that serves your needs.

The example here relates to the local community website that was also featured on page 22.

A SUMMARY LINE EXPLAINS YOUR PROJECT TO YOUR AUDIENCE. IT SUMS UP THE WHOLE VERBAL BRAND.

Example:
"Home to all things quirky and cool in our area."

Use this line frequently in your visual communications. It could also be used as your strapline – a line of text that's always connected to your logo.

SUMMARY LINE/ DESCRIPTOR

FIND A UNIQUE AND MEMORABLE NAME FOR YOUR PROJECT.

Examples:
"Local Connection"
"Neighbours' Network"
"Think Local"

Coming up with a unique name may not be possible, but make sure it differs from other names in your specific sector.

BRAND NAME

BRAND VALUES/ PERSONALITY

SET OUT YOUR PROJECT'S PERSONALITY OR VALUES IN KEYWORDS OR SHORT PHRASES.

Examples:
"We are inclusive."
"We only highlight the positives about our neighbourhood."

This part of the verbal brand is more for you to refer to, rather than to share directly with your audience.

Creating a verbal brand is crucial to a coherent design strategy. It will help you communicate consistently, both verbally and visually, across all communication channels, whether on a website home page, a biography on social media, or an introduction to a printed or digital brochure.

LANGUAGE

COMPILE A STOCK OF KEY WORDS AND PHRASES TO USE ON YOUR PROMOTIONS.

Refer to your tone of voice to help you choose key words and phrases. If words aren't your strong point, consider using a professional copywriter for this key task.

Examples:
"Connecting our community"
"Cool, cultured, connected"
"We love where we live"

BRAND STORY

A BRAND STORY (OR BRAND NARRATIVE) IS WHAT YOU WANT YOUR AUDIENCE TO KNOW ABOUT YOUR PROJECT.

This text is for use on, say, a website home page. Aim for two or three paragraphs – and you will also need a shorter version for use on social media.

Example:
"We're an ever-growing collection of what's best and most fascinating about our neighbourhood – according to us. From cocktails to cuisine and quirky culture, we write about what we like. We celebrate the wonders of our borough, both modern and historic, for the pleasure of everyone, near or far, who shares our love for where we live."

TONE OF VOICE

USE THE SAME TONE OF VOICE TO COMMUNICATE CONSISTENTLY WITH YOUR AUDIENCE.

Your choice of tone of voice will also influence your visual brand: for instance, a chatty tone would probably call for a more informal, casual font style.

Examples:
"We use short sentences."
"We are chatty, but informative."

⌃ ADAPTABLE AESTHETICS

Characterful typography combined with simple graphics results in a friendly logo that works well in any context. The ears of wheat are a nod to the bakery's fair trade ingredients, while the letters seem to rise unevenly like handmade bread in the oven.

DESIGN A **LOGO**

When you design a logo, you are aiming to create a memorable visual symbol for your business or service. The graphic visual language you use tells the story of your brand in its meaning, structure, and visual form.

THE BRIEF

In this case study, a bakery business is in its early stages. The owner has ideas about what they want the brand to be, but they don't yet have a defined identity. Key to developing their brand – which they plan to display across a broad range of media – is to create a recognizable logo.

JOB SPEC:

- Overall aim: to design a logo for a new artisan bakery with shop premises in a local high street.

- Reflect the feel of the brand and appeal to its target audience, considering the following:
WHAT is the main purpose of the business?
WHAT is the brand's personality?
WHO are they trying to attract?
HOW do they want people to feel about the business?

- Stand out from competitors visually and in the message conveyed, as well as on the high street and online.

- Make sure the logo works in a variety of environments and contexts, from product packaging to the shop's signage.

THE TOOLKIT

Once designed, a logo will be at the heart of your design toolkit, but before then, you'll be working with a broader range of ideas. As you research the market, evaluate your competitors, and form your strategy, you should be collecting colours, images, and typefaces. Making a moodboard of these elements can be a great way to focus your brand ideas (*see* page 100). This business owner has already started to think about and collect design elements that will be central to their brand.

MOODBOARD

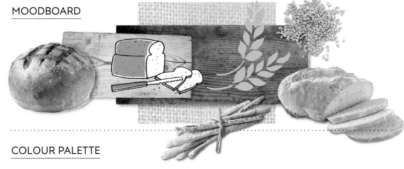

COLOUR PALETTE

BRAND COLOURS

GOLD	BEIGE	BLACK
C0 M26 Y100 K0	C25 M25 Y40 K0	C0 M0 Y0 K100

TYPEFACES

Bokka Half Shadow OT

BETWEEN 1 HEAVY

THE DESIGN PROCESS ≫

DEFINE YOUR MESSAGE

To achieve a logo that fits the brand, you need to be confident of the message you want to convey. Here is the outcome of the brand brainstorm for this project.

SKILLED
FRIENDLY
NURTURING

KEYWORDS TO **DESCRIBE US**

FAIR TRADE INGREDIENTS

OUR BAKERY

WHAT MAKES US **STAND OUT**

ECO-FRIENDLY BICYCLE DELIVERY

ALL PRODUCTS HANDMADE IN SMALL BATCHES

SPECIALIZE IN ANCIENT GRAINS

WHAT DO WE DO?

WHAT ARE OUR **CUSTOMERS** LIKE?

WANT TO SHOP LOCAL

CARE ABOUT THE ENVIRONMENT

WILLING TO PAY FOR CRAFTSMANSHIP

« **BRAINSTORM YOUR BRAND MESSAGE** – SEE PAGE 22

1   2   3

DECIDE ON A STYLE OF LOGO

A logo can be as basic as your company name or initials, or it can incorporate some imagery. When choosing a style of logo, you'll need to consider the business in the context of its market and competitors.

Use a font that chimes well with what the business does

Shorter names are best for wordmarks

The image needs to be unique and recognizable

Simple graphics match well with the font style

Lettermark This logo is made up of one or more letters, usually the initials of the company. If the business has a long name, this can be a useful route.

Wordmark A logo that uses only type, often the company's name, a wordmark can help to create recognition of the brand. This is ideal for a new company.

Image symbol Using a single graphic can be a memorable way to brand a business, though it can be a challenge to find the right image.

Combined mark A combination of type and graphics works hard to reinforce the brand. Keep it simple so it still has impact on a small screen.

THINK ABOUT IMAGERY

Your logo should mean something beyond its design. Any imagery you use can represent a range of meanings, so consider them fully before you commit.

Sign Depicting the product – such as a loaf of bread or croissant – is clear and unambiguous, but an obvious logo may not stand out from the competition

Visual metaphor Images can convey a sense of the brand – a cosy fireside suggests homely comforts, or a chef's hat, craftsmanship. Some ventures lend themselves better to this approach than others.

Wheat was chosen to evoke natural ingredients

Symbol Using an image that symbolizes the business – such as a rolling pin – requires more input from the viewer, but can work well. The chosen logo combines symbols with text to avoid any ambiguity.

» **STYLES OF ILLUSTRATION** – SEE PAGE 110

❯❯ ALTERNATIVE DESIGNS

It's striking how many different options can result from the same brief and colour palette. The font choices in particular have a strong impact on the feel of the brand: some appear classy and formal, others modern and approachable.

CREATE A BRAND THAT STRETCHES

KEEP YOUR BRAND OPTIONS OPEN

You may not envisage ever wanting to expand your brand, but it costs nothing to keep your options open. Thinking about how your brand could cope with expansion might save you a lot of time and money in future. A flexible brand doesn't mean an incoherent one. You can still be consistent whilst creating a brand with stretch. The key is to come up with ideas that connect naturally to your main project. For instance, a pet-sitting business might consider offering garden maintenance to clients on holiday. The business would benefit from the trust it has already built with clients, and make extra money by providing two services at the same visit.

BRAND EXPANSION CHECKLIST

» **Stay true to your brand personality** and values. For instance, a florist thinking of branching out into gifts and greetings cards might decide only to stock those with a botanical or floral theme.

» **Don't change too many brand elements** at once. If you're using a new colour or a different font weight for your extension idea, make sure you keep some familiar elements, such as your existing image style.

» **Keep in mind your verbal and visual brand**. Is your toolkit up to the job of targeting different audiences? You also need to keep hold of your original audience, so it's important to stay consistent in how you promote yourself, from your brand story to your colour palette and logo.

» **Don't create new logos**, unless you really have to. As a general rule, a new product range is more likely to need a new logo. For other brand extensions, such as events, your existing logo can probably be used.

BRAINSTORM A BRAND EXPANSION

To help you brainstorm the possible future demands on the flexibility of your brand, try mapping your ideas on a chart. Draw a large circle and put your project in the centre. Divide the circle into segments, one for each new area you want to explore. Then simply add ideas into the appropriate segment, as you think of them.

NEW PRODUCTS

GIANT CUPCAKES

COCKTAIL FLAVOURS FOR ADULTS

POP-UP AT RAIL STATION

NEW PARTNERSHIPS

It's never too early to think about the future requirements of your brand! Whether you are setting up a project from scratch, or thinking about how to reach a wider audience with your existing venture, the job will be so much easier if your brand is flexible enough to move into new areas without losing its identity.

EXAMPLE:
CUPCAKES TO ORDER
This example looks at a small business, currently operating from home, selling made-to-order cupcakes through a website. The owner might consider expanding by adding seasonal products, hosting workshops, teaming up with a local mobile coffee seller, or targeting customers with special dietary needs.

MAKE A BRAND PLAN

KEEPING TRACK OF PROGRESS

This checklist will help you set out your plan and make sure you're on the right path.

BRAND PLAN CHECKLIST

» Mark out sections
Divide your timeline into three sections: Preparation, Pre-launch and Launch. The Preparation section covers the exercise described on page 14.

» Pre-launch
Divide this section into stages: Research, Verbal, Visual, and Development. These are the points at which you'll be defining and then creating your brand. The exercises on pages 16–39 help to further define these stages.

» Add tasks
Under each stage, add the tasks that need to be completed. If you prefer, use note form rather than full sentences.

» Highlight key information
Highlight key words within your tasks, so you can pick them out at a glance when looking at your finished plan.

» Set yourself deadlines
Allocate a time frame to each stage. Be realistic – much will depend on how much time you can spare, and your budget. The research stage can be particularly time-consuming if you are conducting surveys.

» Set out who else is involved
Keep track of who will be helping you, and when. If others are helping you with the research, assets, or campaign launch, ask them to estimate how much time they will need so you can make provision.

» Pin up the plan
Print your plan as large as possible and put it up where it's easy to view as you work through the stages.

» Update the plan
Add in any new tasks that come up as the project develops. When you finish each task, track your progress by crossing it out or marking it as complete.

PREPARATION

Define your aims and those of your project, then write a project brief.

PRE-LAUNCH

STAGE 1

RESEARCH

INTERVIEW
yourself and colleagues to define what you stand for

DEFINE AUDIENCE
- **Primary research** – surveys, online polls
- **Secondary research** – existing data

AUDITS
- Analyse your existing branding.
- Analyse verbal and visual brands for similar projects or competition.

🕐 DEADLINE:

PEOPLE INVOLVED:

There's a lot to keep track of when creating a brand, and organization is key. Setting yourself deadlines for the different stages and knowing what comes next will help you to focus on current tasks and to keep your eyes on the goal – using your brand to launch a successful project.

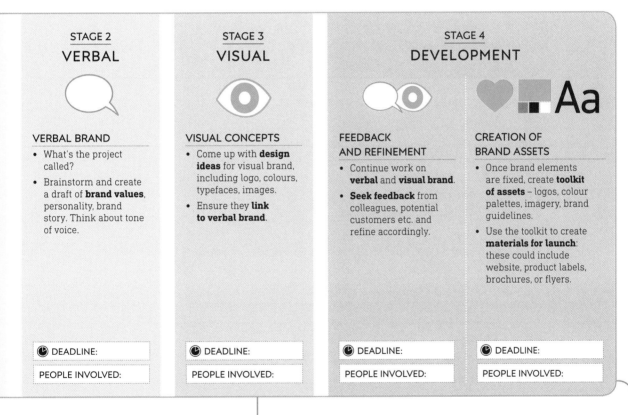

STAGE 2
VERBAL

VERBAL BRAND

- What's the project called?
- Brainstorm and create a draft of **brand values**, personality, brand story. Think about tone of voice.

🕐 DEADLINE:

PEOPLE INVOLVED:

STAGE 3
VISUAL

VISUAL CONCEPTS

- Come up with **design ideas** for visual brand, including logo, colours, typefaces, images.
- Ensure they **link to verbal brand**.

🕐 DEADLINE:

PEOPLE INVOLVED:

STAGE 4
DEVELOPMENT

FEEDBACK AND REFINEMENT

- Continue work on **verbal** and **visual brand**.
- **Seek feedback** from colleagues, potential customers etc. and refine accordingly.

🕐 DEADLINE:

PEOPLE INVOLVED:

CREATION OF BRAND ASSETS

- Once brand elements are fixed, create **toolkit of assets** – logos, colour palettes, imagery, brand guidelines.
- Use the toolkit to create **materials for launch**: these could include website, product labels, brochures, or flyers.

🕐 DEADLINE:

PEOPLE INVOLVED:

LAUNCH!

Once your project launches, the planning stage is over. Your brand enters a new phase where the focus is on promotion, publicity, and creating new materials to keep up interest and attract new audiences. As you become established or expand into new areas, you will need to ensure that you still have the right tools and materials to be able to communicate new information while maintaining your strong identity.

BRANDING WITH LOGOS

| 1 | 2 | 3 |

1. APPLE

The branding genius of Apple – a global tech company revered for the design of its products – is that its logo is instantly recognizable while encapsulating its name in the simplest possible way. The bite out of one side ensures that the symbol is identifiable as an apple at any scale.

2. TWITTER

This logo works both as a tiny favicon – an icon that appears in an address bar – and on a large scale, such as a sign. The bird needs space around it to create a sense of "flight"; it can't be cropped or compromised. Synonymous with a superbrand, it is part of the digital landscape in many countries.

3. NIKE

The Nike swoosh has both the instant recognizability essential for a global brand and the dynamism needed for a sportswear company. The simple, elegant logo suggests positivity and forward motion, which works well on any sportswear product, not least a sports shoe.

4. INSTAGRAM

When Instagram updated its logo from a vintage polaroid-inspired camera to a simplified, rainbow version, it caused uproar. But this modern – and scalable – design, still identifiable as a camera thanks to the "viewfinder" dot, marked the company's shift from photo-filter app to social media monolith.

5. CHANEL

Created by Coco Chanel herself in 1925, the interlocking Cs of Chanel's timeless logo represent its founder's initials. The logo now not only appears on packaging, but is incorporated into the fashion house's luxury products. Its instant recognizability has played a huge role in the success of the brand.

6. THAI AIRWAYS

Initially a predominantly regional airline, Thai Airways updated its classical "dancing man" logo in the mid-1970s to appeal to its increasingly international base of customers. The new design, refreshed in 2005, incorporates the gold of Thailand's temples and the rich colours of its orchids and silk.

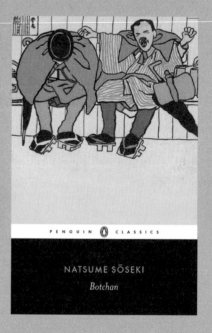

| 7 | 8 | 9 |

7. FERRARI

Ferrari's badge – a shield on race cars – is highly symbolic. The black horse (a tribute to fighter pilot Francesco Baracca) suggests power and speed; yellow symbolizes Modena, Enzo Ferrari's birthplace; and his nationality is represented by the green, white, and red of the Italian flag.

8. WWF

The lovable charm of WWF's logo communicates the environmental organization's key message beyond any language barrier. Despite several evolutions – including the addition of the organization's name in 1986 – WWF's panda remains an icon of the conservation movement.

9. PENGUIN

"Dignified, but flippant" is how Penguin's name was originally described, deemed appropriate for its inexpensive but good quality books. The publisher's characterful logo was designed in the same spirit and its first appearance on Penguin's simple covers made the brand immediately recognizable.

10. IKEA

The bold colours and heavy font of the Swedish furniture company's logo are unarguably impactful. Changing dramatically through several iterations since 1951, the brand's now world-famous blue and yellow – representing the national flag – weren't added until 1983.

11. FEDEX

The type in the FedEx logo – a combination of Univers and Futura bold – has been cleverly manipulated to communicate a subliminal brand message: the negative space between the "E" and the "x" forms a white arrow, suggesting speed, efficiency, and precision.

12. ILLY

Coffee company illy took its logo from a specially commissioned artwork by James Rosenquist – an American artist working in the pop art movement – in 1996. Five stylized white "brushstrokes" depict the brand's name, capturing what it considers the "art" of making espresso.

BUILDING BLOCKS }

TYPE
O**48**

COLOUR
O**70**

IMAGE
O**90**

TYPE

Type describes the characters and letterforms that designers use to convey language – and typography is the art of using type in a conscious way to convey a message or meaning. Typography gives the designer incredible powers of communication, so learning how to recognize, choose, and use type to suit your projects and aims is essential. And as you grow in confidence, you'll be comfortable enough with the rules to be able to branch out and break them if you need to.

MATCH FONTS TO MOOD }

ONE WORD, MANY MOODS

Type is a powerful tool. Often without us noticing, it projects a mood that profoundly affects our response to the words we read. The structures and forms that make up a typeface and help define its personality are explained later in this chapter, but first, here is a simple exercise to show how type alone can set a tone.

Imagine that each of these "Announcement" headings precedes a different message. Try matching each heading to one of the events listed below. There's no right or wrong – use your judgement to decide which heading is the best fit for the mood of the message you want to convey:

» Notice of a train cancellation
» Birth of a baby
» Flyer for an antiques fair
» Theatre group auditions
» Memorial service
» 30th birthday party invitation

Announcement }

GILL SANS MT PRO 32PT

A typeface like this projects a cool, detached persona. Its understated presence makes it versatile and adaptable.
Typeface classification: Humanist sans serif
Also try: Frutiger, Myriad Pro, Verdana

Strokes of the same width give a uniform effect

Announcement }

PERPETUA REGULAR 36PT

With its discreet, decorative flourishes, this typeface has a traditional, almost official air. It looks and feels authoritative and serious.
Typeface classification: Transitional serif
Also try: Minion, Caslon, Garamond

Characters are made up of both thick and thin strokes

Announcement }

LEMON TUESDAY 34PT

Echoing the flowing forms of hand-written lettering, text like this conveys an informal, friendly mood.
Typeface classification: Script
Also try: Snell Roundhand, Brush Script

Varied line widths appear spontaneous, like handwriting

The role that type plays in design is much more complex than just being a means to convey words clearly to the reader. Every typeface has its own personality and projects a specific character – choose wisely to set the right mood and tone for your design project.

NEUTRAL
UNDERSTATED
PRACTICAL

QUIRKY
WHIMSICAL
FUN

{ *Announcement*

CURLZ MT REGULAR 33PT

FORMAL
SERIOUS
POLITE

Swirls lend characters
an eccentric air

Some typefaces convey a subtle mood while others, such as this lighthearted and quirky example, make a more immediate impact.

Typeface classification: Display

Also try: Rosewood, Aftershock, Jokerman

ASSERTIVE
ASSURED
FORTHRIGHT

{ Announcement

ITC LUBALIN GRAPH BOOK 26PT

PERSONAL
STYLIZED
APPROACHABLE

Chunky, rectangular
decorative blocks catch
the reader's attention

The forms that make up this typeface project self-confidence and attention-grabbing style.

Typeface classification: Slab serif

Also try: Clarendon, Memphis, Rockwell

RETRO
SOPHISTICATED
ELEGANT

{ **Announcement**

BRAGGADOCIO REGULAR 21PT

Stylized forms like this were
a feature of the art-deco art
movement of the early 20th century

Some typefaces evoke nostalgia by nodding to the past. The forms of this typeface seem to offer a whiff of 1920s' European café culture.

Typeface classification: Display

Also try: Time Machine, Arnold Boecklin

ANATOMY OF A TYPEFACE

THE STRUCTURE OF TYPE

Learning the anatomy of type will help you to identify similarities and differences between different typefaces so you can choose the right typeface for your project.

INVISIBLE FRAMEWORK

To ensure that all the characters work together well, a typeface is usually designed around a framework of horizontal lines, rather like a musical stave.

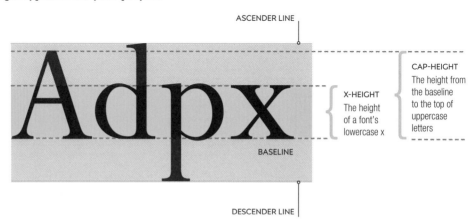

ASCENDER LINE

CAP-HEIGHT
The height from the baseline to the top of uppercase letters

X-HEIGHT
The height of a font's lowercase x

BASELINE

DESCENDER LINE

JARGON-BUSTER:
TYPEFACE OR FONT?

These terms are used interchangeably almost everywhere but technically, there is a difference between the two.

Typeface describes a whole family of characters, regardless of size or style, that share the same design features.

Font describes a set of characters within the typeface that share a style.

So, for example: Palatino is a **typeface**, whereas Palatino Bold is a **font**.

TYPE ANATOMY

The terms used for the marks that make up type can vary: here are some of the most common usages.

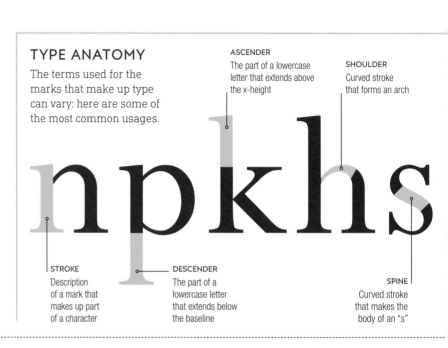

ASCENDER
The part of a lowercase letter that extends above the x-height

SHOULDER
Curved stroke that forms an arch

STROKE
Description of a mark that makes up part of a character

DESCENDER
The part of a lowercase letter that extends below the baseline

SPINE
Curved stroke that makes the body of an "s"

Put simply, "type" describes the non-handmade letterforms that we produce to make the words that convey our languages. A basic grasp of how type is constructed is the first step in mastering typography, which is the art of arranging type to suit its context, and the bedrock of all good design.

LETTER CASE

While most fonts offer uppercase and lowercase versions of their characters, some specialized display fonts may only be available in a single case.

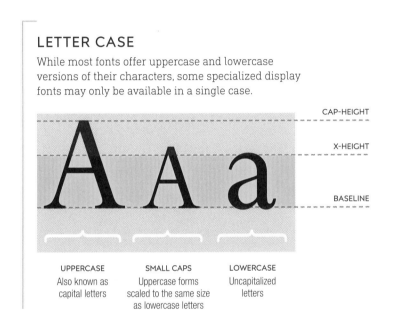

CAP-HEIGHT

X-HEIGHT

BASELINE

UPPERCASE
Also known as capital letters

SMALL CAPS
Uppercase forms scaled to the same size as lowercase letters

LOWERCASE
Uncapitalized letters

LIGATURES

Some typefaces offer ligatures, where two letterforms are combined to make a new, single form.

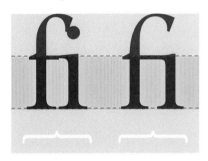

SEPARATE LETTERS
The "f" and "i" characters clash unattractively when next to one another

LIGATURE
A ligature makes the two characters into one, avoiding a clash

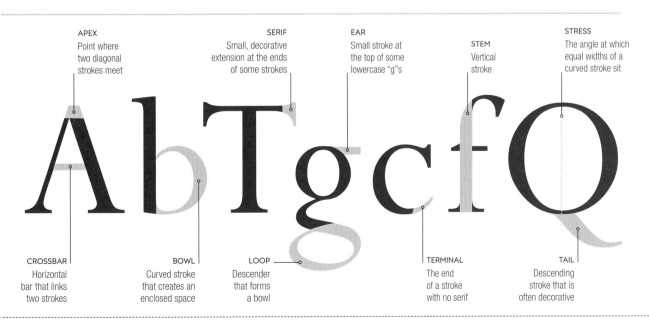

APEX
Point where two diagonal strokes meet

SERIF
Small, decorative extension at the ends of some strokes

EAR
Small stroke at the top of some lowercase "g"s

STEM
Vertical stroke

STRESS
The angle at which equal widths of a curved stroke sit

CROSSBAR
Horizontal bar that links two strokes

BOWL
Curved stroke that creates an enclosed space

LOOP
Descender that forms a bowl

TERMINAL
The end of a stroke with no serif

TAIL
Descending stroke that is often decorative

MEASURING TYPE }

THE ORIGINS OF TYPE MEASUREMENT

Many of the ways we measure type developed from the early days of printing, when typefaces consisted of individual blocks of metal, each representing a character in the font. For instance, the way we measure the size of a font derives from the height of these blocks. Each size of letter had to have its own complete set of blocks.

PERPETUA 100PT METAL TYPE BLOCKS

POINT SIZE

Point size is the size of a font, including the space taken up by its uppercase letters, ascenders, and descenders.

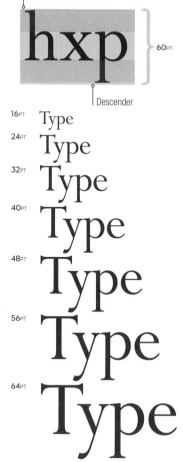

Ascender

60PT

Descender

16PT Type
24PT Type
32PT Type
40PT Type
48PT Type
56PT Type
64PT Type

X-HEIGHT

The x-height measurement helps a designer gauge how big a font will look in use. Fonts of the same point size but different x-heights can look very different when set in a block of text.

PERPETUA
REGULAR 35PT

HELVETICA NEUE
ROMAN 35PT

The quick brown fox jumped over the lazy dog. The quick brown fox jumped over the lazy dog.

PERPETUA 12PT

Fonts with a small x-height leave breathing space between lines of text

The quick brown fox jumped over the lazy dog. The quick brown fox jumped over the lazy dog.

HELVETICA NEUE 12PT

Larger x-heights are easier to see, but take up more space so text looks more dense

The size of letterforms and their position in relation to each other have a huge influence on the look and readability of text. Here are some of the main methods designers use to measure and adjust type.

LEADING

Leading is the term for the space between lines of text. It is usually set so that a font's ascenders and descenders do not touch.

Space increases or decreases when leading is adjusted

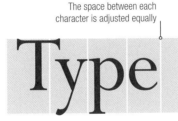

PERPETUA 22/32 — Notation means that type size is 22pt and leading is 32pt

The quick brown fox jumped over the lazy dog. The quick brown fox jumped over the lazy dog. The quick brown fox jumped over the lazy

PERPETUA 12/12

Ascenders and descenders are almost touching at this setting

The quick brown fox jumped over the lazy dog. The quick brown fox jumped over the lazy dog. The quick brown

PERPETUA 12/16

Increased leading prevents clashing and allows type room to "breathe"

TRACKING

Also known as letter-spacing, tracking describes the spacing between the characters in a word, line, or paragraph of text.

The space between each character is adjusted equally

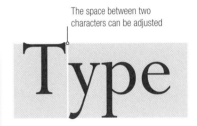

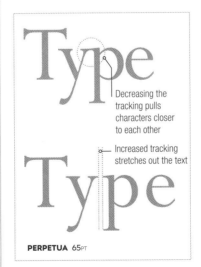

Decreasing the tracking pulls characters closer to each other

Increased tracking stretches out the text

PERPETUA 65PT

TRACKING GUIDELINES

Designers use tracking mainly to improve the readability of text. Take care not to overdo tracking; characters that overlap or are too far apart can make text harder, not easier, to read.

KERNING

Kerning is the process of adjusting the space between individual characters, so that a word appears more evenly spaced.

The space between two characters can be adjusted

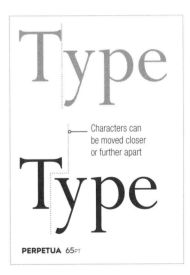

Characters can be moved closer or further apart

PERPETUA 65PT

KERNING GUIDELINES

Kerning is particularly useful for headings or logos, where the visual impact of a word is crucial. Kerning can make a word look more balanced and easier to read.

GROUPS AND CATEGORIES OF TYPEFACE

SERIF

Typefaces in this category share the common feature of small extensions, known as serifs, which appear at the ends of some of their strokes.

SANS SERIF

These typefaces are defined by their lack of serifs – "sans" in French means "without". Letterforms are deliberately plain, with no flourishes or decoration.

TRANSITIONAL

This style's main features are high contrast between thick and thin strokes, and curved serifs. The stresses in rounded strokes are at a near-vertical angle, known as semi-oblique.

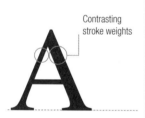

Contrasting stroke weights

Stress

Tapering serif with flat base

TIMES REGULAR 90PT

Useful for: Longer texts. Well-proportioned x-height and short ascenders and descenders make this style highly readable, particularly in small point sizes.

Also try: Baskerville, Perpetua

MODERN

Developed from the transitional serifs, modern styles share an extreme contrast between thick and thin strokes and their serifs are geometrical and flat, not curved. Stresses are vertical.

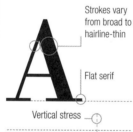

Strokes vary from broad to hairline-thin

Flat serif

Vertical stress

BODONI LT PRO 90PT

Useful for: Grabbing or holding a reader's attention. Striking letterforms have visual impact, although they can be hard to read when used small. A popular style for logotypes.

Also try: Didot, Walbaum

GROTESQUE

The first sans serifs to be produced, grotesque typefaces are neutral and consistent, with simple geometric forms and little variation in stroke width.

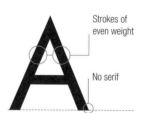

Strokes of even weight

No serif

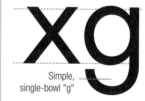

Simple, single-bowl "g"

FUTURA 90PT

Useful for: Headings and logotypes. This style works well in different contexts, but tall x-heights and lack of stroke contrast can make smaller sizes hard to read.

Also try: ITC Franklin Gothic, Helvetica

HUMANIST

A dominant style in the 20th century, this group presents a clean, uncluttered look, while keeping some of the calligraphic forms of old-style serif typefaces, such as the double-bowl "g".

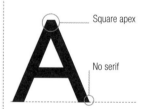

Square apex

No serif

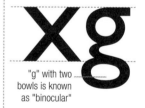

"g" with two bowls is known as "binocular"

GILL SANS 90PT

Useful for: Extensive sections of text. Many families have strong distinctions between weights, making it easy to create contrast and keep readers' interest in a large or complex layout.

Also try: Myriad Pro, Verdana

Although you don't need to be an expert in the history and classification of type, learning some of the broad categories will come in handy when, faced with a bewildering array of typefaces, you are trying to make a choice.

SCRIPT

Many typefaces are directly modelled on hand-formed letters, from the intricate lettering of medieval scribes to the flowing strokes of modern calligraphy.

BLACKLETTER

Also known as Gothic script, the earliest printed typefaces mimicked the broad-nibbed heavy, angular style of hand-lettering that was common in the 15th century.

Thick and thin bars mimic pen strokes

Tight spacing between letters

FETTE FRAKTUR 90PT

Useful for: Large-size headings or logos, especially to convey a distinct visual, cultural or historical mood or message.

Also try: Fraktur, Lucida Blackletter

SCRIPT AND CURSIVE

These typefaces aim to capture the fluency of handwriting. Styles range from formal to casual, and lowercase forms either link together (script) or are unjoined (cursive).

Right-sloping strokes mimic handwriting

Long, flowing descenders

PRISTINA 90PT

Useful for: Headings and short texts that need to look friendly or personal, such as invitations. Legibility can be an issue if point size is small or line spacing is tight.

Also try: Mistral, Caflisch Script, Alex Brush

SLAB SERIF

Also known as Egyptian styles, these typefaces emerged in the 19th century, along with the era of mass-produced goods. They were designed purely to grab attention – and sell. Serifs are large and heavy, often the same weight as the strokes.

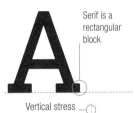

Serif is a rectangular block

Vertical stress

DIN NEXT SLAB 90PT

Useful for: Large headings and advertising. Slab serifs work best in large sizes. Their strong personality can clash with other fonts; they pair best with more understated styles.

Also try: Memphis, Rockwell, Sentinel

DISPLAY

Display typefaces are designed purely for large headings or short messages. They tend to have highly stylized, eccentric letterforms. Display font families are small – often they have only one or two weights, and some are only available in upper case.

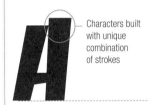

Characters built with unique combination of strokes

Strokes end at varying heights

Highly stylized letterform

BANCO ITC HEAVY 90PT

Useful for: Making a statement at a large size, for instance on a poster. Display fonts are never used for normal running text.

Also try: Cooper Black, Avant Garde, Marker Felt, Ultra Gotham, Museo, VAG Rounded

USE TYPEFACE FAMILIES

KEEP IT IN THE FAMILY

In a typeface family, the variations all share some basic characteristics, such as x-height, length of ascenders and descenders, or the shapes of certain characters.

ABCDEFGHIJKLMNOPQRSTUVWXYZ
abcdefghijklmnopqrstuvwxyz 1234567890
!@£$%^&*()_+-=;"<>?,./

HELVETICA ROMAN

In every typeface family, there is a basic font from which all the variations are derived. As in the case of the Helvetica family shown on this page, the base font is usually Roman.

WEIGHTS

A typeface's weight describes how thin or thick its strokes are. Some families feature lighter or heavier weights than Helvetica, the family shown here.

LIGHT WEIGHTS

Thinner strokes allow more white space in and around each letterform, lending a generous, spacious feel to the font.

MID WEIGHTS

These weights are designed so that their spacing is most appropriate for easier reading. Roman, also known as Regular, is the basic style of the family, and the one most often used for longer text.

HEAVY WEIGHTS

With increasingly thicker strokes, the letterforms' bowls become smaller, reducing the white space that makes reading easier. Spacing between characters is adjusted at these weights, so that the text does not become too dense.

As weight increases, space between and within characters decreases

Helvetica Ultra Light
Helvetica Thin
Helvetica Light

Roman is the standard weight in a type family

Helvetica Roman
Helvetica Medium
Helvetica Bold
Helvetica Heavy
Helvetica Black

With so many typefaces available, it's tempting to use all your favourites in one design. But finding the right type combinations can be tricky and time-consuming. Using a single typeface with many variations can be a good solution, providing consistency while still delivering plenty of visual contrast.

FORM AND WIDTH VARIATIONS

Most conventional type families offer every weight in either Roman (upright characters) or italic (sloping characters). Some families also allow a choice of the width of characters.

ITALICS

Also known as oblique styles, these tilted letterforms are used mainly for emphasis, or to denote a word from another language within a text.

HELVETICA NEUE **ITALIC** ULTRA LIGHT – BLACK

CONDENSED

Also known as narrow or compressed, these fonts are useful for headings, as you can use a larger point size while taking up minimal horizontal space.

HELVETICA NEUE **CONDENSED** ULTRA LIGHT – BLACK

EXTENDED

Extended (also known as wide or expanded) fonts can make punchy headings, but as with condensed styles, readability can be an issue.

HELVETICA NEUE **EXTENDED** ULTRA LIGHT – BLACK

OTHER VARIATIONS

Some type families include quirky display fonts for headings. Here, Helvetica Bold has been rendered in outlines.

HELVETICA NEUE **BOLD** OUTLINE

TYPE SUPER-FAMILIES

Typeface families used to consist of variations within a single type classification, such as sans serif. However, the new "super-families" offer sub-families from two or more categories. Some also feature greatly expanded character sets, so designers can choose from a selection of alternatives for many of the font's characters.

Although styles vary, letterforms remain consistent

DIN NEXT REGULAR

DIN NEXT STENCIL

DIN NEXT ROUNDED REGULAR

DIN NEXT SLAB PRO REGULAR

DIN NEXT SHADOW BOLD

DIN NEXT SLAB RUST BOLD

CHOOSE THE RIGHT FONT FOR THE JOB

WHERE WILL IT BE SEEN?

Start by listing all the different formats in which your text will be seen and testing them out on each. Fonts can behave very differently at different sizes, and what looks eye-catching and fun on a poster could be an unreadable mess on a tablet or phone.

One, two, three, four, five, six, seven, eight, nine, ten, eleven, twelve, thirteen.

Georgia is a serif font designed for low-resolution readability

SMALL-SCALE

For small printed text, a serif is often best, but on small screens, the serifs can clog together. Consider a dedicated webfont or a simple sans-serif.

Helvetica's letterforms are instantly readable

READ me quickly as you pass by...

LARGE-SCALE

A billboard is usually read quickly from a moving vehicle, so type has to be absolutely clear. Simplicity is key – think before opting for a quirky, big-personality display font.

WHO IS THE AUDIENCE?

Some readers have specific physical or other requirements that you need to take into account, especially when choosing a font for body copy – that is, longer blocks of text.

One, two, three, four, five, six, seven, eight, nine, ten, eleven, twelve, thirteen, fourteen

GARAMOND REGULAR 10/12PT

GENERAL READERS

For most adults, a Roman serif, with point size of 9 or 10 and leading at 12, makes for the easiest read.

One, two, three, four, five, six, seven, eight, nine, ten, eleven

GEORGIA REGULAR 11/13PT

OLDER READERS

Eyesight deteriorates with age, so for older readers, consider increasing the point size and using a font with larger letterforms.

One, two, three, four, five, six, seven, eight, nine, ten, eleven, twelve, thirteen, fourteen, fifteen

DIN NEXT LT PRO CONDENSED 10/12PT

TEENAGERS

Light text on a dark background (reversed-out text) is impactful but tiring to read. Only use for readers with no eyesight issues.

Aa is for... apple

FUTURA BOLD/BOOK

CHILDREN

New readers can find it hard to decipher more unusual letterforms. Go for typefaces with regular, geometric forms that most children will already be familiar with.

Futura's simple forms make it popular for children's books

When choosing a typeface, perhaps the most important consideration is the mood it evokes. But there are other, practical factors to take into account, too. Asking yourself a few basic questions about the job you need the text to do will help you to narrow the field and pick the best font for the task in hand.

HOW WILL YOU USE **NUMBERS**?

In a typeface, numbers are usually either aligning ("lining") or non-aligning ("oldstyle"). Aligning numbers are all the same height and align along the font's cap height. Non-aligning numbers are more decorative, with some dipping below the baseline or finishing above the cap-height line

Numbers all align at cap-height line and baseline

A1234567890

DATE OF BIRTH: 16/01/1995

ALIGNING
Use aligning numbers for tables, forms, and when pairing numbers with capitals.

HELVETICA NEUE THIN

Some numerals extend beyond cap-height line and baseline

A1234567890

He was born on 16th January 1995, at 4.30pm.

NON-ALIGNING
Use these numbers within text, when they are in sentences alongside lowercase characters.

ADOBE GARAMOND PRO ITALIC

DO YOU NEED **SPECIAL SYMBOLS**?

Special characters, called glyphs, are included in many fonts. Depending on the project, you might need copyright and trademark signs, maths symbols, or characters with accents for different languages. Some fonts offer purely decorative symbols, called type ornaments, which can be a useful (and cost-effective) way to get illustrative features into your designs.

π©Ω™®{}§¶»

HELVETICA NEUE ROMAN

HARRY WELLS

Piano Teacher

HARRY WELLS

Piano Teacher

Exam tuition

·

All ages and levels welcome

·

Free taster session

07777 123123

harry@wellsmusic.net

BUSINESS CARD

Your next lesson...

Date	Time
Date	Time
Date	Time
Date	Time
Date	Time
Date	Time
Date	Time
Date	Time

HARRY WELLS

Piano Teacher

APPOINTMENT CARD

47 Park Avenue, Northtown NN19 1BP
07777 123123 | harry@wellsmusic.net

LETTERHEAD

SLEEK AND SIMPLE

A piano motif is the main graphic feature of each component of this stationery suite. Combined with the name and job title centred underneath, it forms a simple logo, easily transferable to all communications materials. The turquoise background of the cards is reduced to a strip on the other stationery, providing another visual link between all the items.

HARRY WELLS

Piano Teacher

47 Park Avenue, Northtown NN19 1BP
07777 123123 | harry@wellsmusic.net

with compliments

COMPLIMENTS SLIP

DESIGN BUSINESS **STATIONERY**

Every venture, no matter how small-scale or digitally oriented, needs to communicate in print. A suite of stationery with a unified identity projects a professional image that inspires your audience to have confidence in you.

THE BRIEF

A self-employed music teacher needs practical and professional stationery that he can use in his micro-business. He hasn't yet thought about branding.

JOB SPEC:

- Overall aim: to develop a suite of useful communications materials that will reflect well on this micro-business. The materials needed are: letterhead paper, a business card, an appointment card, and a compliments slip.

- For each item, determine the following and compose an appropriate design:
HOW can it convey the nature of the business?
WHAT is the specific purpose of the item?
WHAT practical information needs to be included?

- There should be consistency across the suite to create a co-ordinated visual identity for the business.

- The design should be flexible enough to work in the different formats required.

THE TOOLKIT

If you are just starting up or are operating a micro-business, you may not have a toolkit of design materials yet, so this could be your first opportunity to think about your venture's image. If so, it can help to find a starting point around which you can make other design choices. This may be a visual motif, a particular typeface, or a colour palette. For this project, there was no existing brand identity, but the business owner had sourced an image of a piano to be the focus.

GRAPHIC DEVICE

A business card is a tiny canvas, so any images or graphics need to be simple. This piano silhouette – a copyright-free image sourced online – will be recognizable even at very small sizes.

COLOUR PALETTE

BRAND COLOURS

TURQUOISE
C72 M0 Y22 K0

BLACK
C0 M0 Y0 K100

Adding colour to your stationery will make it look more professional and create a stronger reaction in your audience, but keep it minimal. Check with your printer about the options and pricing available to you.

TYPEFACES

Bickley Script Com

Madera light

Madera Medium

Madera Bold

THE DESIGN PROCESS

DESIGN THE BUSINESS CARD FIRST

The core item is the business card – it's what most people see first, so needs to make an impact. It may be cheaper to print on only one side, but two-sided printing gives you more space to work with. Formats vary, but they generally include the options below.

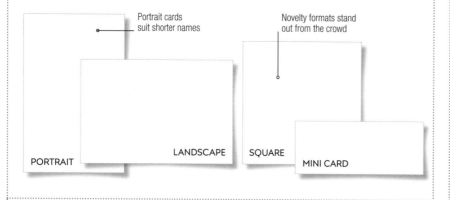

Portrait cards suit shorter names

Novelty formats stand out from the crowd

PORTRAIT

LANDSCAPE

SQUARE

MINI CARD

LETTERHEAD AND COMPLIMENTS SLIP

Stationery for correspondence needs to have a simple design so it doesn't take up space needed for the content. You also need to consider text size carefully; it shouldn't draw too much attention away from the content, but it still needs to be legible. As a general rule, make sure your font is no smaller than 9PT.

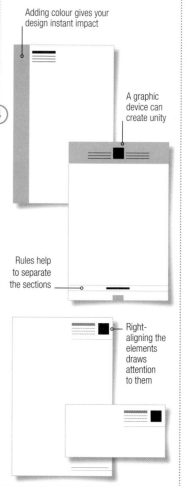

Adding colour gives your design instant impact

A graphic device can create unity

Rules help to separate the sections

Right-aligning the elements draws attention to them

① ② ③ ④

FIND A PRINTER

Whether you use an online or local print shop, your printer can advise on sizing, as well as the type and weight of paper. They can supply templates like this to help you position elements correctly.

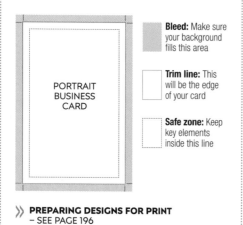

PORTRAIT BUSINESS CARD

Bleed: Make sure your background fills this area

Trim line: This will be the edge of your card

Safe zone: Keep key elements inside this line

» **PREPARING DESIGNS FOR PRINT** – SEE PAGE 196

DECIDE ON STYLE

The feel and finish of your stationery creates a strong impression, so ask your printer what's available. For cards, unusual corner styles are a quick and easy way to stand out.

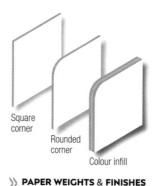

Square corner

Rounded corner

Colour infill

» **PAPER WEIGHTS & FINISHES** – SEE PAGE 206

›› ALTERNATIVE DESIGNS

This selection shows that, even with the most basic brief, there is plenty of scope for a variety of design approaches. As with the main project, each business card will form the basis for the rest of the suite.

›› INSTANT IMPACT

A square format immediately sets this card apart. It works particularly well with a powerful graphic, such as this keyboard, which neatly describes the business.

Turquoise rules add the only accents of colour in a monochrome design

⌃ TYPE AND COLOUR

This card is simplicity itself: it demonstrates how colour and type alone, skilfully handled, can create striking and memorable designs. The rounded edges give it quirky finish.

Black and orange colourway is reversed on either side of the card

⌃ LEADING LINES

A clear visual link between front and back of the card is essential: here, a musical stave provides continuity and also makes an useful framework for the text.

COMBINE TYPEFACES FOR IMPACT

WHY USE MORE THAN ONE FONT?

Using only one font is rather like wearing only one colour – when you add in a second, accent shade, the contrast adds spark to the first. Contrasting type also helps the reader to distinguish the different kinds of copy, which in turn makes it easier to follow meaning.

DIFFERENT ROLES

Using a different font can make it clear to the reader that here is a different kind of information, for instance if you are attributing a quote, or adding a picture caption on a page of text.

> "You cannot open a book without learning something."
>
> CONFUCIUS

NAVIGATION AID

Marking sections with headings in an eye-catching font helps readers find their way round a page. Short, decorative headlines set a style that reflects personality, while the body copy font is functional and readable.

Desserts and coffee

Sticky toffee pudding
with vanilla ice cream or custard   £6

Chocolate brownie
with candied ginger and chocolate sauce   £6

ADD TEXTURE AND INTEREST

It is the graphic designer's job to tempt an audience into picking up – and sticking with – the text. Blocks of copy in different styles add visual texture, helping the reader glide effortlessly through the whole story.

Interesting facts are highlighted by pulling them out of the text and giving them a different style. Interesting facts are highlighted by pulling them out of the text and giving them a different style Interesting facts are highlighted by pulling them out of the text and giving them a different style Interesting facts are highlighted by pulling them out of the text and giving them a different style Interesting facts are highlighted by pulling them out of the text and giving them a different style Interesting facts are highlighted by pulling them out of the text and giving them a different style Interesting facts are highlighted

Interesting facts are highlighted by pulling them out of the text and giving them a different style.

INTRODUCE DRAMA

Setting up a contrast between conventional type and a showy font can inject drama. Here, the meaning of the sentence is boosted by a font that evokes the look and feel of old-style comic books.

He fell in with a giant...

Contrast plays a huge role in all aspects of graphic design, and particularly when it comes to type. Sometimes it's not possible to create enough contrast or drama with just one font or type family – you need a combination. Follow these guidelines for font pairings that work every time.

FINDING GOOD COMBINATIONS

Successful font combinations are largely a matter of trial and error, of putting fonts together and judging the effect. Here are some basic guidelines and a few pairing suggestions to get you started.

FONT COMBINATION CHECKLIST

(1) OPPOSITES ATTRACT

Aim for fonts that complement or contrast. Pairing a serif with a sans serif is a good place to start if you're new to combining fonts.

(2) GIVE ONE FONT TOP BILLING

When pairing, let one or other font dominate. Giving them equal billing can cause the fonts to conflict, rather than work as a team.

(3) DON'T USE SIMILAR FONTS

Avoid fonts that look very similar. Readers may assume they are seeing a single font, and be thrown off by the tiny differences they perceive.

(4) LESS IS MORE – USUALLY!

Be restrained. Start with two fonts, and only add more if you really need to. You want to achieve clarity and harmony, not type soup!

(5) ASSIGN ROLES AND STICK TO THEM

Be consistent – make a list of the roles you have assigned to each font, and apply it throughout your design. For example, your style list might look like this:

Headings: Font A (Bold 36PT)
Body text: Font B (Roman, 10/12)
Captions: Font C (Italic, 9/12)

GARAMOND
+ Helvetica Neue Roman

GARAMOND/HELVETICA NEUE ROMAN

A classic serif/sans-serif pairing, this combination teams an elegant, easily readable heading with clean, simple, and equally legible text.

TRADE GOTHIC
+ Sabon Roman

TRADE GOTHIC BOLD/SABON ROMAN

The two typefaces contrast with one another in weight and style, while their similar x-heights mean they combine well to create text that's approachable and readable.

PERPETUA
+ Gill Sans Regular

PERPETUA/GILL SANS

Both these fonts are the work of Eric Gill, so it's no surprise that they team up well. Both are based on the classical forms that inspired Gill's work as a stonemason and type designer.

USE TYPE GRAPHICALLY

MATCHING FORM AND MEANING

An effective way to enhance the meaning of type is to set a word or phrase in a way that visually describes it. This technique both reinforces what is being communicated and turns type into an eye-catching graphic.

① featherweight

② **heavy**

③ p a n o r a m a

④ CROWDED

⑤ tiny

⑥ HUGE

⑦ UP

1 An ultra-light font reflects the meaning of the word. **2** Slab-like serifs appear to weigh down the characters. **3** Wide spacing can make text harder to read, so use with care. **4** Reduced letter spacing squeezes the word to create visual tension. **5** and **6** Lower- and uppercase letters, scaled appropriately, illuminate the words' meaning. **7** A visual pun uses the direction of type to make a joke – the word UP literally goes up.

⑧ **FADING AWAY**

⑨ DISTANCE
DISTANCE
DISTANCE
DISTANCE
DISTANCE

⑩ **RED**
ALERT!

⑪ PATTERN PATTERN

8 Gradually reducing the tint of each character produces a fade effect. **9** Repeating a word at increasing sizes creates a sense of depth and perspective. **10** Coloured type emphasizes the warning. **11** The same word repeated in grid formation creates a textured pattern.

Typography is the art of arranging text to make its message as clear and accessible as possible. One useful way of achieving this is to take advantage of the graphic qualities of type, setting it in a way that enhances both its meaning and its visual impact.

WORDS AND FRAMES

Type doesn't exist in a vacuum: it interacts with other text, and with the frames and graphics around it. Manipulating these relationships to create "word graphics" can illuminate or add to the sense of text.

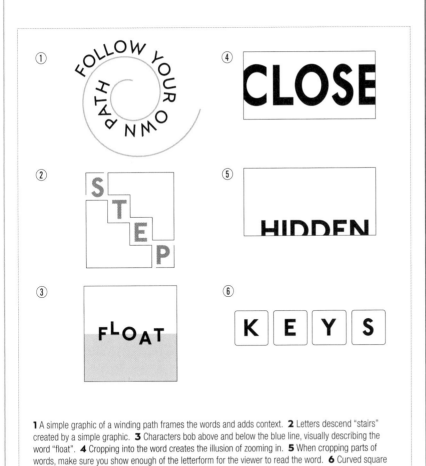

1 A simple graphic of a winding path frames the words and adds context. **2** Letters descend "stairs" created by a simple graphic. **3** Characters bob above and below the blue line, visually describing the word "float". **4** Cropping into the word creates the illusion of zooming in. **5** When cropping parts of words, make sure you show enough of the letterform for the viewer to read the word. **6** Curved square frames around the letters suggest a keyboard.

CRIMES AGAINST TYPE!

Most design software allows you to distort words or letters, changing their scale or angle. Distortion can be used to make a one-off visual point but should never be used to alter the look of text designed for reading – the result will be ugly and often unreadable. **Never use distortion to style blocks of text – use condensed, extended, or italic fonts instead.**

The examples below were made by manipulating this word:

DISTORTED

JOHNSTON ITC PRO MEDIUM 25PT

DISTORTED

The angle of the text frame has been set at 30°. The letterforms, while still recognizable, look malformed when compared to their original shape.

DISTORTED

Here, the horizontal scale of the word is reduced to 30% of its original width. This extreme compression has narrowed some of the strokes so much they would be invisible at small sizes.

DISTORTED

If the vertical scale is set to 30%, the eye has to work quite hard to make sense of the word – D and O form similar shapes.

COLOUR

Colour is the lifeblood of graphic design. Understanding the meanings that we apply to colour is a good start, but it is up to you to express the specific values of your project or brand by mastering this powerfully expressive tool. To use colour confidently, you'll need to understand what colour is and how it works, know how to choose and use palettes to suit your project, and get to grips with how colours operate differently when used in print or digital forms.

THE PSYCHOLOGY OF COLOUR

HOW COLOURS MAKE US FEEL

Humans react powerfully on an emotional level to colours. Research has shown that there is consistency in the responses people have to colours: for example, warmer colours (red, orange, yellow) generally stimulate, while cooler colours (blue, indigo, violet) are calming. Designers choose colours to elicit a reaction in their audience that will chime with the message. However, many other factors can influence an individual's reaction to colours in a design, so colour psychology is only one factor to consider when choosing a palette.

THE SYMBOLISM OF COLOURS

Although interpretations vary hugely, colour is used all over the world to symbolize collective values. Red, for instance, means love and passion to many, but is also the colour of blood, conflict and revolution. In China, red is the luckiest colour, whereas in South Africa it is worn by mourners. In the West, a red light is a warning and a "red rag to a bull" a provocation to anger. The most common values ascribed to colour are shown here, but designers should always look carefully for any specific associations their target audience might have.

PINK	RED	ORANGE	YELLOW
EMPATHETIC	EMPOWERED	ENTHUSIASTIC	WARM
HOPEFUL	PASSIONATE	ENERGIZED	POSITIVE
CALM	ENERGETIC	CONFIDENT	STIMULATED
NURTURING	**ALERT**	**SOCIABLE**	**HAPPY**
BEAUTY	**LOVE**	**CREATIVITY**	**CURIOSITY**
SENSITIVITY	STRENGTH	PLAYFULNESS	CLARITY
FEMININITY	DANGER	COURAGE	WISDOM
ROMANCE	HEAT	YOUTH	COWARDICE

When you design with colour, keep in mind both the emotions that different colours evoke, and also the meanings and values that different communities and cultures attach to them. The right colours in the right place will invigorate the design and help the audience to connect with the message.

GREEN	BLUE	PURPLE	BROWN	WHITE	GREY	BLACK
GROUNDED	PURPOSEFUL	INSPIRED	COMFORTABLE	YOUTHFUL	STEADY	SELF-CONFIDENT
REFRESHED	SECURE	CREATIVE	SERIOUS	HOPEFUL	COMPOSED	
OPTIMISTIC	TRUSTING	INDULGENT	RESILIENT	DETACHED	NEUTRAL	NEGATIVE
TRANQUIL	**PEACEFUL**	**SPIRITUAL**	**SAFE**	**REJUVENATED**	**REFLECTIVE**	**POWERFUL**

GREEN	BLUE	PURPLE	BROWN	WHITE	GREY	BLACK
LUCK	**SUCCESS**	**ROYALTY**	**NATURE**	**PURITY**	**INTELLIGENCE**	**MYSTERY**
FERTILITY	POWER	WEALTH	SOLIDITY	SINCERITY	CONFORMITY	AUTHORITY
NAÏVETY	CONFIDENCE	WISDOM	MASCULINITY	STERILITY	OLD AGE	EXCLUSIVITY
JEALOUSY	CONTROL	MYSTICISM	SADNESS	PERFECTION	BALANCE	MOURNING

UNDERSTANDING COLOUR }

WHAT IS COLOUR?

Colour does not exist in darkness. Light – which travels in waves – gives colour to our world and the objects within it. White light is made up of waves of different lengths; which colours we see depends on the wavelengths of light that reach our eyes. An object looks a certain colour to us because its surface absorbs some wavelengths and reflects others. For example, a banana looks yellow because it reflects only yellow light – all the other wavelengths are absorbed by its surface.

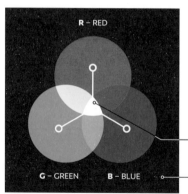

R – RED

G – GREEN   **B – BLUE**

RGB
ADDITIVE COLOURS

DIGITAL COLOUR – RGB MIXING

The colours on digital screens are made by emitting and mixing different proportions of red, green, and blue light. The more colours you add, the brighter the new colour will be. A mix of all three colours results in white. This additive-mixing model is known as RGB, from the initials of the three base colours.

Red, green, and blue lights combine to make white

Black represents a screen not emitting any light

M – MAGENTA

C – CYAN   **Y – YELLOW**

CMYK
SUBTRACTIVE COLOURS

PRINTED COLOUR – CMYK MIXING

As with the banana example above, paints or pigments and inks applied to any surface create colour by absorbing, rather than emitting light. Combinations of cyan, magenta, and yellow make new colours by reducing the range of wavelengths that they reflect – the more colours in the mix, the darker the colour. This subtractive method of mixing is known as CMYK, from the initials of its base colours, plus "K", which stands for black.

The three pigments combine to make black

White represents paper with no ink

DESCRIBING COLOURS

In design, specific terms are used to describe the ways in which colours are manipulated to achieve different effects.

HUE

This describes the named, separate colours of the spectrum, such as red. Each hue is distinguished by its wavelength.

TINT

Tints are lighter versions of a hue. They are achieved in different ways, depending on whether colour is RGB or CMYK, but the result looks the same to a viewer.

SHADE

Mixing a hue with black makes a darker version, known as a shade. Shades are also widely referred to as tones.

TONAL VALUE

This describes the specific qualities of a hue, including its evenness, brightness, or depth. Tone operates independently of colour: when a hue is converted to black and white, its tone is preserved.

HALFTONE
Different-sized black dots create varying tones of grey

DUOTONE
A hue plus black, or two tints of the same hue, create a duotone image

When creating a visual identity for your projects, it's helpful to have a basic grasp of colour and how it looks and behaves in different media, and to learn some of the most common terms used to describe the colour variations that you can create.

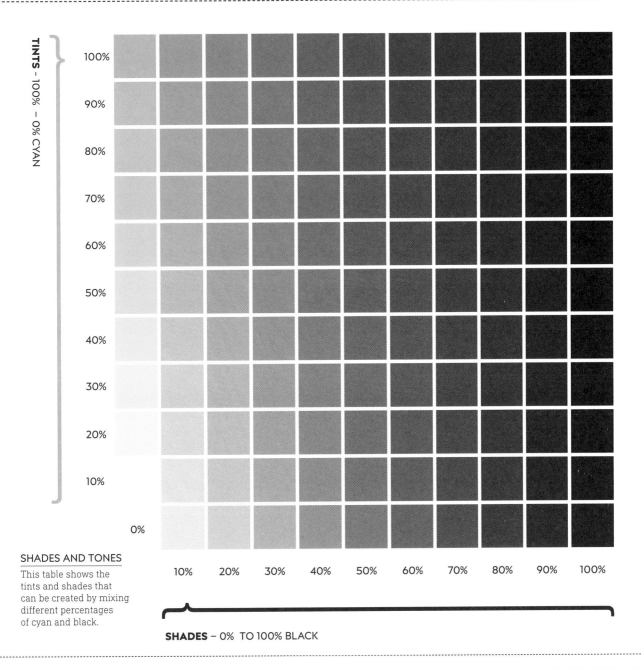

TINTS - 100% – 0% CYAN

SHADES AND TONES

This table shows the tints and shades that can be created by mixing different percentages of cyan and black.

SHADES – 0% TO 100% BLACK

USE THE COLOUR WHEEL

COLOUR WHEEL THEORY

Light can be split into constituent colours by passing it through a prism. The spectrum can then be expressed as a 12-section wheel that shows how the colours relate to each other. The closer two colours are, the more they will harmonize when put together. The further they are from each other, the greater the contrast will be.

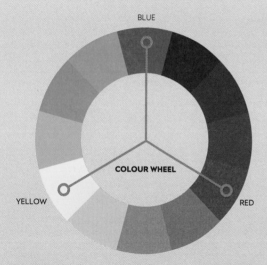

BLUE

COLOUR WHEEL

YELLOW

RED

PRIMARY

Blue, red, and yellow are the three primary colours. They are so called because they cannot be mixed from other colours.

SECONDARY

Green, orange, and purple are secondary colours. They sit between the two primaries that were mixed to create them.

TERTIARY

Mixing a primary with its nearest secondary makes a tertiary colour. They slot between the colours that created them.

IDEA 1

CLEAR CONTRAST

One way to make an impact is by using contrast – and colours that sit directly opposite each other on the wheel provide maximum contrast. Placed together, each colour makes the other appear brighter and more vibrant.

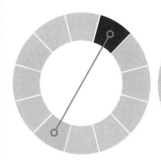

CONTRASTING PAIR

Colours at opposite points of the wheel are complementary. Pairings such as dark blue/yellow-orange create an energizing effect. Take care using these pairings with type. Colours can "vibrate" next to each other and make text difficult to read.

TEAM OF FOUR

Four colours arranged as complementary pairs are known as tetradic. A scheme like this gives scope for variation, but balancing strong contrasts requires care. Experiment with making one colour dominant and using the others as accents.

The colour wheel, which shows how different colours relate to each other, will be familiar if you've studied art or physics. It's also a useful tool in graphic design, helping you compare colour combinations to decide which you want to use – and which are best avoided.

IDEA 2
PERFECT BALANCE

When choosing a working colour palette, three can be the magic number. You can give each colour equal billing, but it's often more useful to choose one colour as your major theme with the other two in a supporting role.

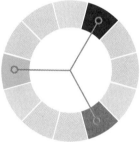

SUBTLER CONTRAST

Team a colour with the two on either side of its complement to create a split-complementary scheme. This creates harmony as well as contrast. Blue contrasts with the two other colours, while yellow and orange, close together on the wheel, provide harmony.

BALANCED TRIO

Colours that are equally spaced are known as triadic. This combination uses every fourth colour on the wheel – here, blue is teamed with lime green and orange. Find the best balance by trying different combinations of dominant and accent colours.

IDEA 3
HARMONY OF HUES

For a rich, unified feel, pick a palette made up of colours that sit next to each other on the wheel. Whether you choose two, three, or even four colours, you can be sure that they will work to create a harmonious whole.

COOL COMBINATION

Analogous combinations generate maximum harmony and minimum contrast. Here, dark blue is combined with its two neighbours, primary color blue and blue-green, from the left-hand side of the wheel. This creates a cool, tranquil colour palette.

WARMER TONES

If you take the same dark blue starting point and team it with purple and deep pink from the right side of the wheel, you create a warmer palette. Here, the blue star seems to take on the warmth of its neighbours – for more on how colours interact, see the next page.

HOW COLOURS INTERACT }

COLOUR IN CONTEXT

A colour never appears in isolation; even a white background will influence how you perceive it. The chart on the right shows how colour looks different depending on the hues it is adjacent to. In design, you can use the ways that colours interact to create an impact on page or screen. You should, however, be careful when using type on coloured backgrounds – some combinations can make your text extremely difficult to read. If in doubt, avoid using coloured text type – save colour for display headlines.

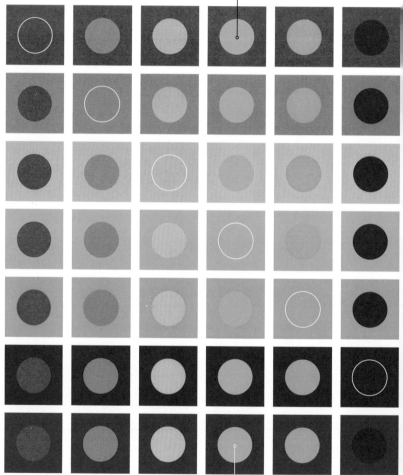

Green and red are opposites on the colour wheel, but their similar tones make them jar when put together

The green squares on the right appear lighter than those on the left, but they are exactly the same. The blue background mutes the value of the green, while the yellow boosts it.

The chart maps out how colours can appear to take on a different hue or value depending on their background.

Green and purple contrast strongly and have different tonal values, so they combine in a pleasing way

Colour is not fixed or consistent – we perceive it differently depending on its context or surroundings. Understanding how colours interact with each other will help you use colour with maximum impact in your designs.

Black and dark blue have little contrast and similar tones, making the pairing a poor choice for text on a background

COLOUR VIBRATION

When contrasting colours with a similar tone or value (brightness) are placed next to each other, the result is a glowing effect, sometimes known as vibration. While this effect can result in eye-catching designs, it can feel aggressive to the viewer, particularly on screen. Strongly vibrating combinations should not be used for type, as it makes text extremely hard to read.

RED/GREEN TYPE COMBINATIONS

The contrasting colours here vibrate so strongly that the brain is tricked into seeing movement that isn't there.

DIFFERENT VIEWERS

How colours look also depends on who is looking at them. People with colour blindness, for example, cannot see the difference between certain colours. The condition also narrows a viewer's perception of tone and shade. To make sure your designs are accessible, you can make use of various free apps that simulate different types of colour blindness so you can check what others may see.

SPECTRUM SEEN WITH NORMAL VISION

SPECTRUM SEEN WITH RED-GREEN COLOUR BLINDNESS

Colour-blind viewers cannot see a number

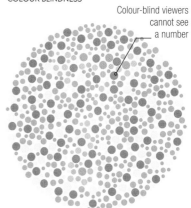

Consider colour-blind audiences by adding labels or icons instead of conveying important information via colour alone.

BARHOLM HIGH SCHOOL

Summer Fair

SUNDAY 23 JUNE

10AM – 4PM **ENTRY: £2 PER FAMILY**

BBQ • PUPPET SHOW
GLITTER TATTOOS
FACE PAINTING
CRAFT STALLS
DESIGN YOUR OWN
ICE-CREAM SUNDAE

MAIN PLAYING FIELD

12PM PET TALENT SHOW
2PM   PARENTS VS. TEACHERS
      RELAY RACE
3PM   CHILDREN'S FANCY DRESS

REGISTER 30 MINUTES BEFORE
THE START OF EACH EVENT!

BARHOLM SCHOOL PLAYING FIELDS
HOPE STREET, BARHOLM, BM19 1DY

ALL PROCEEDS TO BARHOLM SCHOOL FUND

SUNDAY FUN DAY
A combination of disciplined text hierarchy, a simple layout, and careful choice of graphics and colours gives this complex poster a real sense of fun.

DESIGN A **LARGE POSTER**

To connect with their moving targets, posters must quickly grab attention and deliver the headline message. Secondary information should be conveyed in a clear and structured way to solicit engagement and minimize reader effort.

THE BRIEF

A school would like to promote their fundraising fair this summer to encourage people to attend and to raise money.

JOB SPEC:

- Overall aim: to design a poster to advertise a school's summer fair and communicate the event details without diluting the poster's main purpose or overwhelming the audience.

- Convey all relevant information clearly and concisely:
  WHAT is the event?
  WHERE is it taking place?
  WHEN is it happening?
  IS THERE an entry fee?
  WHAT activities can be enjoyed?
  WHAT participatory events are happening and how can people get involved?

- The key headline information must be easily legible from a distance and in passing.

- Give a flavour of the event experience by conveying a sense of summer and family fun.

THE TOOLKIT

Always check if an organization has any devices that should be featured, such as a school crest. Then, focus on bringing the key information to life by deploying an armoury of typefaces and fonts, getting creative with colour, and making imaginative use of graphic devices. For this project, there were no brand guidelines to follow or logos to build the design around: simply a list of the information to be included.

GRAPHIC DEVICES

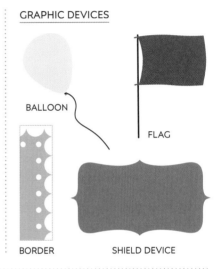

BALLOON

FLAG

BORDER

SHIELD DEVICE

COLOUR PALETTE

GREEN	BLUE	PINK	PURPLE	YELLOW	BLACK
C20 M0 Y70 K0	C60 M0 Y20 K0	C0 M45 Y35 K0	C50 M70 Y0 K0	C0 M0 Y70 K0	C0 M0 Y0 K100

TYPEFACES AND FONTS

DIN Next LT Pro Light

DIN Next LT Pro Medium

DIN Next LT Pro Black Condensed

Artane Elongated BT Regular

Tartine Script Pro Bold

THE DESIGN PROCESS

GROUP THE INFORMATION

Start by dividing the information into different groups. These groups will need to be styled differently to help the audience find them easily. This poster has been grouped in the following way:

1. Event name
2. Event host
3. Date, time, price
4. Attractions/stalls
5. Schedule of events
6. Practical information

① SUMMER FAIR

② Barholm High School

③ Sunday 23 June
10am–4pm
£2 per family

⑤
12pm Pet talent show

2pm Parents vs. teachers relay race

3pm Children's fancy dress

Be there 30 minutes before the start to register!

④
BBQ
Puppet show
Glitter tattoos
Face painting
Craft stalls
Design your own ice-cream sundae

⑥
Barholm School Playing Fields, Hope Street, Barholm, BM19 1DY

THINK ABOUT THE HEADING

Most readers will engage with the poster only briefly – unless you grab their attention. Make the heading the most dominant feature and build the rest of the design around it.

Size: Making the heading text the biggest instantly signifies its importance.

Colour: A heading in coloured type stands out from the black and grey text in the rest of the poster.

Decorative device: Enclosing the heading in a border adds to its visual impact.

« **USE COLOUR TO CREATE ORDER** – SEE PAGE 144

———— ① ———————————————————— ② ———————————————————— ③ ————

USE HIERARCHY TO STYLE GROUPS

Skilful use of tools such as typography and spacing, or graphic devices like borders or coloured panels, will help the audience to distinguish the different sections of text.

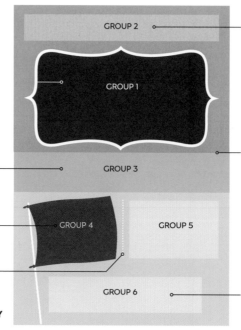

Group 2 has a prominent position but is smaller than the heading

The heading is set in a script font to show it is in a group of its own

Close spacing shows that the heading and text below it should be read together

A coloured band encloses group 3, in which all the text is centred

Group 4 is contained within a graphic device

A vertical line divides groups 4 and 5

Groups 4, 5, and 6 – attractions, events and venue information – share the same green panel

Centred text at the bottom forms another group

« **CREATE ORDER WITH TYPOGRAPHY** – SEE PAGE 142

›› ALTERNATIVE DESIGNS

Both these designs apply an emphatic visual theme and reflect slightly different choices in the ranking of information. They also demonstrate a contrasting use of text alignment: all text is centred in one poster, while the other uses mainly left alignment and justification to help organize its information.

⌃ BLUE-SKY THINKING

The dominant blue colour and cloud graphic promise a fine day for this fair. The design gives greater prominence to the list of activities through the strength of type, the "blockiness" of the justified alignment, and the position of the green band, which straddles the centre of the layout.

⌃ MELTING IN THE HEAT

The graphics and colour palette of this design are strongly themed around ice cream, evoking summer, seaside, and 1950s vintage style. As on the original poster, the heading type is on a curve – always check the spacing between letterforms, evening out gaps that may make the text harder to read.

MAKE YOUR OWN COLOUR PALETTE

GETTING STARTED

Digital technology makes it easy to sample and get data on colours you find in photos or online. Here are some easy steps to putting together your own colour palettes.

① REFER TO YOUR EXISTING DESIGN ELEMENTS

If you are researching for a specific project, and have already collected elements such as a logo, photos, or rough design, keep them handy so you can refer to them.

② BROWSE FOR INSPIRATION

When you are reading books and magazines or browsing online, look out for colour schemes that you find effective. Inspiration could come from an article on interior design, a work of art, or the colour theme of a website. You need a digital image to make a palette, so photograph, scan, or take screen grabs of things you want to keep.

③ RECORD THE WORLD AROUND YOU

You can also take your own pictures of eye-catching colours you encounter. You could be inspired by the colours of, say, a local beauty spot or a friend's choice of outfit.

④ FIND A COLOUR-PICKER TOOL

You can get data on the colours in digital images by using a colour picker: this is a tool that's included in most design software. Free tools are also available online – search "colour picker". A picker allows you to select an area of an image and then gives you information on its colour make-up.

⑤ PICK A PALETTE

Use the picker tool to select different colours within your image, until you have put together a palette of three or more that you think work together well. To check how well your colours relate to each other, you could use an online guide – search "colour guide tool" to find a selection of apps.

⑥ SAVE THE COLOUR VALUES

Once you have a palette you like, save the colours and their values – this is the technical information on each colour's make-up that you need to recreate them. Colour values are expressed as RGB, Hex, or CMYK codes; RGB and Hex are used for digital design, while CMYK is used for print media.

SAMPLING AN IMAGE

A picker tool is used to create a palette from the colours that make up the vibrant pattern on the butterfly's wing.

MAIN PALETTE

1	2	3	4
C80 M0 Y35 K0	C20 M5 Y100 K0	C80 M0 Y85 K0	C0 M0 Y0 K100

ACCENT COLOUR

5
C10 M85 Y70 K0

This notation shows the CMYK values – the percentages of cyan, magenta, yellow, and black that makes up each colour

The colour palette – a collection of colours used for a project or brand – is a key component of any project's design toolkit. Build up a collection of your favourite colour combinations by taking inspiration from your surroundings, and from images of nature, travel, fashion, or art.

SPRING PASTELS

C10 M10 Y15 K0	C20 M35 Y20 K0	C40 M45 Y30 K15	C65 M30 Y15 K0

NEUTRALS AND ACCENTS

C20 M10 Y20 K0	C50 M40 Y20 K5	C65 M15 Y100 K0	C0 M85 Y45 K0	C90 M65 Y50 K55

MUTED AND NATURAL

C15 M5 Y20 K0	C30 M15 Y40 K0	C30 M10 Y75 K0	C60 M30 Y60 K20	C95 M30 Y35 K15

EARTHY AND VIBRANT

C20 M25 Y50 K5	C0 M35 Y95 K0	C35 M50 Y65 K35	C10 M95 Y85 K0

COLOUR IN POSTERS

München ◯◯◯◯◯ 1972

OTL AICHER

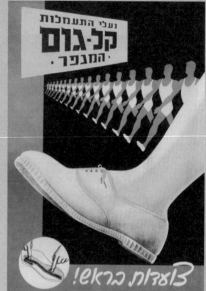

ISRAELI SCHOOL

THEOPHILE STEINLEN

1. BLOCK AND BLEND

Using only blues and greens, Otl Aicher achieved a striking dynamism for this 1972 poster for the Munich Olympics by mixing block colour with more subtle blending. In contrast, the Olympic rings appear reversed out in white.

2. HIGH CONTRAST

With a typical 1950s asymmetrical composition, this Hebrew shoe advertisement uses contrasting colours to draw the eye to the product. The receding line of figures echoes the angle of the shoe, both pointing to the heading.

3. SIMPLE PALETTE

Created in 1896, this poster promotes *Chat Noir* (Black Cat), a French cabaret troupe. Using just three colours, the design is dominated by the eponymous cat, its arresting golden eyes echoing the colour of the background.

PAUL RAND

VELVET CREATIVE OFFICE

WALDEMAR SWIERZY

4. A PLAY ON PICTURES

This 1982 poster for US
computing giant IBM takes a
playful approach by using visual
puns to spell out the company
name. The flat expanse of black
leads the eye to the graphics at
the centre of the space.

5. BERLIN IN BLUE

One of a series advertising the
Berlin film festival, this poster
features the city's bear mascot atop
the Brandenburg Gate. The wash
of vibrant blue, combined with
an unusual angle, give the iconic
landmark a fresh, modern feel.

6. LIGHT AND DARK

This 1956 Polish poster advertises
the Italian film *Villa Borghese*.
Its combination of dark vertical
and lighter horizontal stripes
work together cleverly to suggest
that the figures are walking –
or perhaps hiding – among trees.

4	6
5	

7. BOLD BAUHAUS

Designed by Joost Schmidt for the first exhibition of the Bauhaus group – radical artists and designers – in 1923, this poster caused a sensation with its bold, geometric forms, block lettering, and limited, high-contrast colour palette.

8. PURE AND SIMPLE

Malcolm Grear's 1969 poster is typically modern and almost as iconic as the museum it promotes. Evocative of screen printing, the reversed-out white suggests the swirling shapes of the Guggenheim Museum in New York, USA.

9. PSYCHEDELIC SWIRLS

Produced in 1964 to promote the opera *Wozzeck* in Poland, rippling lines of red and pink chime with the work's theme of emotional turmoil and disorientation, and are reminiscent of *The Scream*, by Edvard Munch.

ALEKSANDER RODCHENKO

GIOVANI PINTORI

TADINORI YOKOO

MASSIMO VIGNELLI

10. RED ALERT

This 1925 poster, designed to promote literacy in the USSR, is typical of the visual style of Soviet propaganda at the time. It combines bold colours with simple geometric shapes and expressive, graphic typography.

11. COLOUR IN MOTION

This poster of 1953, designed by Giovanni Pintori for Italian firm Olivetti, features a colourful explosion of lines that jump from letter to letter, suggesting the rapid movement of a typist's fingers over the typewriter keys.

12. CULTURAL SYMBOLS

Artist Tadanori Yokoo produced this 1968 poster for an art exhibition. A comic take on traditional Japanese motifs, it features a fish dripping with paint and flat colours and numerals suggestive of painting-by-numbers.

13. PLAYFUL LAYERING

The bright typography in Massimo Vignelli's 1967 poster for design firm Knoll is made to appear transparent, creating a kaleidoscope of vivid colours and a bold, clean-cut look that is emblematic of the legendary designer's style.

IMAGE }

Whether it's photos, hand-drawn illustrations, or digital artworks, images are core components of graphic design. Everyone can snap a photo, but getting the most from photography takes forward thinking, from setting up a home photo shoot to knowing how and when to buy in photos you need. Illustration can add so much to design work – use it to tell a compelling story, visualize complex information, or simply to inject wit or warmth.

Photography

Illustration

USE PHOTOGRAPHY IN DESIGN

WHY USE PHOTOGRAPHS?

Whether you want to describe a product, set a mood, build a relationship with the viewer, or tell a story, a well-chosen photograph will often do the job with more precision and eloquence than even the best copywriter. Here are some of the ways to use photography to convey a powerful, authentic message.

The product is in sharp focus, with no distracting background detail

This knitter shows off one of her own creations, her direct gaze conveying approachability

The product is enhanced by carefully chosen props and expert lighting and styling

SELL A PRODUCT

If you are offering any kind of product for sale, a photo of it is almost always the best way to go. Composition and lighting should be arranged to give the viewer the clearest picture of what they are potentially buying.

ESTABLISH TRUST

A good portrait or team shot can be a really effective way to convey the personal side of your project. Putting a human face to a business helps a customer to remember you, and builds trust in your setup.

CREATE AN IDEAL WORLD

A professionally styled photo carries an aspirational message: *if you owned this product, this could be your lifestyle!* Creating photos like this can be complex and costly, but they are a powerful way to reinforce a brand story.

In this online age, photography plays a huge role. Through social media, photos are now the main means of communication and self-expression for many people. Understanding how to use photos is a key part of the graphic design skill set.

HOW TO GET THE PHOTOS YOU NEED

Essentially, there are three options for sourcing photos. Thinking about your photography needs and wants will help you choose between them.

DIY PHOTOGRAPHY

A cost-effective option is to take your own photos. You don't have to spend time briefing someone, and the DIY option also gives you scope to experiment and be more creative. Bear in mind that you might have to invest in new equipment, and the job will probably take you more time than it would a professional (see page 94, Choose and use photo equipment).

HIRING A PROFESSIONAL

Using a pro is often the low-stress route to high-quality photos. Professional photography does not come cheap though, so you need to be sure that the return on the photos will justify your spend (see page 204, Working with professionals).

STOCK IMAGES

Maybe the picture you need already exists. For instance, if you want a single photo of a sunflower field in Provence, it's cheaper and easier to obtain one that has already been taken, rather than fly there yourself or commission a professional. There are plenty of sources of low-cost and even free images (see page 210, Finding design resources).

A photo reassures the audience, so they know what to expect

Shooting from a high angle shows the technique clearly while giving the image depth

TELL A STORY

Photos showing what you offer, such as yoga classes, or the place where you make your product, help the audience to understand your project or brand. On websites and social media, you could consider using videos to do the job.

TEACH A TECHNIQUE

A photo is a good way to convey practical information, such as how to adjust bicycle gears. How-to photographs need to be clear and informative – there's no room for innovative camera angles and moody filters with this type of shot.

CHOOSE AND USE PHOTO EQUIPMENT

LIGHTS...

Unless you have professional studio lights and the expertise to use them, natural light is your best bet – it gives subjects an even, 3D quality. However, a few inexpensive essentials in your toolkit can make a big difference when you work with natural light.

TRIPOD

A tripod keeps the camera steady when you use a slower shutter speed in low light. It also ensures consistency if you are taking a series of product photos, enabling you to shoot from the same angle and distance each time.

REMOTE SHUTTER RELEASE

A remote release, used with a tripod, ensures the camera is still while shooting. Remotes are available for most cameras, including phones. Try also using a remote for portraits – your subject will relax more when you are not crouched behind the lens, issuing instructions.

LIGHT REFLECTOR

A reflector is one of the simplest and best ways to boost available light, bouncing it back onto your subject. Reflectors are cheap to buy, or you could use a piece of white card or foam board.

DIY PHOTO STUDIO

The trick to shooting in natural light is to maximize the available light, and to make that light as even as possible, to minimize shadows and dark areas in your photos.

DIY PHOTO STUDIO

For this setup, you'll need the following:

- Two chairs
- A roll or sheet of clean, uncreased white paper
- Bulldog clips
- Sheet of white card
- Tracing paper or sheer curtain

Place the chairs close to a large window, positioning the reflector card to bounce as much light as possible back onto the subject, so both sides of it are evenly lit. Place the tripod and camera in front of the subject and use a remote shutter release for maximum sharpness.

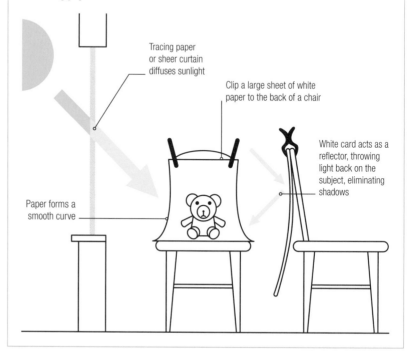

Tracing paper or sheer curtain diffuses sunlight

Clip a large sheet of white paper to the back of a chair

White card acts as a reflector, throwing light back on the subject, eliminating shadows

Paper forms a smooth curve

If you're starting out, you will probably be taking your own photos to use in your work. You can easily spend a fortune on photography equipment, but with just a few wise buys and a little know-how, you can really improve the quality of your shots.

... CAMERA...

Before you shell out on a more elaborate camera, it's worth trying what you have available. If you are photographing small items on a plain background, a good-quality phone camera could well be up to the job.

PHONE CAMERA
If you use a phone camera, check the settings and make sure you are shooting in the highest possible resolution. You might only need a small image now, but one day, your photo might be on a billboard.

COMPACT CAMERA
Also known as a point-and-shoot camera, its main advantages over the phone are its ability to zoom without losing quality, and a more powerful, sophisticated flash. Compact cameras also have a longer battery life than phones, making them a safer bet when shooting on location.

DIGITAL SINGLE LENS REFLEX (DSLR)
The most expensive choice, a DSLR has fully manual controls and detachable lens attachments. This makes it the most versatile camera to use, and for specialist tasks, such as macro (extreme close-up) photography, a DSLR is essential.

... ACTION!

If you are using a phone or point-and-shoot camera, all you have to do is tap the screen to focus the camera on your subject. With a DSLR camera you have more flexibility; settings can be adjusted in different conditions or to achieve a variety of effects. There are three main variables to get to grips with:

SHUTTER SPEED
The shutter opens to let light into the camera sensor. Shutter speed measures, in fractions of a second, how long the shutter takes to open and close. If the light is good, use a fast shutter speed for a sharp image. In low light, you need to leave the shutter open for longer, which can result in blurring, especially if the subject is moving.

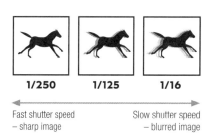

Fast shutter speed – sharp image   Slow shutter speed – blurred image

APERTURE OR F-NUMBER
The aperture is the size of the hole that the shutter makes when it opens. Aperture size is measured in f-numbers and determines how much of an image is in focus – the depth of field. A large f-number means that a large area of the image is in focus. With a small f-number, only the subject is sharp – everything around it is blurred.

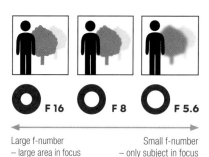

Large f-number – large area in focus   Small f-number – only subject in focus

ISO
The ISO number measures the camera's sensitivity to light. The higher the ISO, the more light-sensitive the sensor becomes, allowing you to take pictures in lower light conditions. Be cautious, though, as very high ISO settings can produce grainy, poor-quality images.

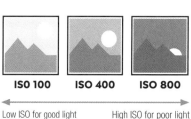

Low ISO for good light – lots of detail   High ISO for poor light – less detail

TAKE PICTURES WITH IMPACT

COMPOSING PHOTOS

Composition is all about how the shapes, tones, and colours of an image are arranged. The way you balance these three elements within the frame of your photo is often the difference between a good and bad photo. Here are some tips for cracking compositions.

HORIZONTAL OR LANDSCAPE FORMAT

VERTICAL OR PORTRAIT FORMAT

The lighthouse, at the lower left intersection, draws the eye into the image

Many cameras can be set to show the grid while you shoot

FIT THE FORMAT TO THE SUBJECT

Let your subject dictate which way you hold the camera. For instance, a skyscraper taken horizontally could leave "dead space" on each side. Turning the camera to vertical fills the frame with the subject – and highlights the building's tall, slender form.

USE THE RULE OF THIRDS

Many photographers and artists use a composition tool called the rule of thirds, where the image area is divided into a nine-square grid. Placing points of interest where grid lines meet can produce a dynamic, balanced composition. For more on using this rule, see page 133.

CONSIDER THE BACKGROUND

Throwing the background out of focus is a good way to put the emphasis on your subject. Set a wide aperture on your manual camera, or, with a phone, shoot as close as possible to the subject or use an app that blurs backgrounds as you shoot.

USE LINES TO LEAD THE EYE

Diagonal lines are powerful devices in composition, leading the eye from one area to another. Here, the lines of the railway tracks lead you to the group of people. They then continue past the group and converge in the distance, hinting at the remote location and of long journeys that await.

You've got your camera and equipment, you've chosen a subject, and you're all ready to shoot. Now all you have to do is construct a picture that's appealing, impactful, and most importantly, perfect for your design.

SHOOTING TO FIT YOUR DESIGN

It's one thing to create a good photo, but bear in mind that your image will need to work within your design. For instance, will your photo cover the whole page, with words superimposed on top? Or will it form part of a complex layout, surrounded by type?

LEAVE ROOM FOR TYPE

If you are planning to place text directly on areas of your photo, it's much better to shoot with this in mind, than to spend time and energy later retouching your image. Leave clear areas so your type will show up well. If you aren't sure about your final design, give yourself options by leaving plenty of space all round the subject. Later, you can crop the image or change its format to suit your design.

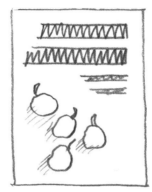

Make a rough sketch to map the position and proportions of images and text.

Your background should be plain and even-toned, so any type placed on it is readable.

INTEGRATING WORDS AND IMAGES

A "cutout" is created by removing the background of an image using photo-editing software. The shape of the subject then becomes the frame of the image. Cutouts are an effective way to break up long text. They add organic shapes to a layout, rather than just another rectangle.

Shoot the subject on a plain white background to make it easier to cut out.

The boundary of the new image follows the shape of the object

Use editing software to cut away the background and define the image's new shape.

In your layout, the text will wrap itself around the contours of the cut-out image.

CROP AND EDIT IMAGES

CROPPING IMAGES

Cropping is the term for cutting away parts of a picture. Most photo-editing software gives you the option to crop images, either retaining the image's orginal proportions or creating a new format or shape.

GOOD CROP...

It isn't always possible to compose the perfect picture while you are shooting – cropping gives you the option to improve an image after the fact. With a phone camera, cropping is a better bet than using the zoom, which can result in poor-quality, pixelated images.

... BAD CROP

As with many photo-editing tools, the crop tool is best used with restraint. Over-cropping can make an image look unbalanced or diminish its impact and meaning.

DON'T LOSE THE CONTEXT
Sometimes, you need the bigger picture. Here, zooming in shows more detail of the surfer, but completely loses the context of man versus gigantic, awe-inspiring wave.

BOOST EMOTIONAL APPEAL
Cropping close in on faces makes an instant emotional impact. With babies, it's much better to crop after the event than to risk tears by looming in too close!

FOCUS ON WHAT MATTERS
Cropping can improve a composition by trimming away any messy details that distract the viewer, allowing the most telling part of the image to fill the frame.

AVOID AWKWARD AMPUTATIONS
Beware of chopping off body parts. A good general rule when photographing people is to avoid cropping bodies at the joints, especially the ankle, knee, or wrist.

Digital photography allows you to amend and improve images in all kinds of ways after the shot has been taken: you can boost the exposure, make an image sharper, or add filters and special effects to transform an image's mood or meaning.

EDITING AND RETOUCHING

There are apps that allow you to change images in all kinds of ways. Altering contrast and colour can boost a picture's impact. Remember, though, that editing can't turn a bad picture into a good one – always start with a high-quality, sharp, and well-composed image.

ORIGINAL

INCREASED CONTRAST

BRIGHTENED

BRIGHTNESS/ CONTRAST

If an image is dull or dark, you can boost contrast or brightness.

Take care that lighter areas don't look bleached

WARM COLOUR FILTER

POSTERIZED

COLOUR

Adjusting the balance of colours can make an image appear more natural, or do the opposite and create a striking special effect.

BLACK AND WHITE

GREEN DUOTONE

SATURATION

Removing colour is known as desaturation. Once an image is desaturated, you can add selective colours back to make sepia or other tones.

ADDING AND TAKING AWAY

Extending or erasing parts of an image can make it more useable.

EXTENDING THE BACKGROUND

If an image has an area of solid colour, such as the sky, you can extend the area to change the format or make space for type.

Flags have been removed, leaving the sky area clearer

DELETING MATERIAL

Most editing packages allow you to retouch areas of an image. This is useful if you need to clear an area – for instance, to make type more readable.

MAKE A PHOTOGRAPHY MOODBOARD

Creating a moodboard is a good way to find your own photographic style. Whether you put items on a pinboard or compile a digital one, collecting inspiring items provides focus and clarity. This board was created to help a jewellery maker decide how best to photograph her work for an online shop.

① ITEMS OF JEWELLERY TO PHOTOGRAPH

MOODBOARD CHECKLIST

This list of themes will help you as you gather items for your moodboard. Don't be too critical at this stage – include anything that appeals and seems relevant.

① THE SUBJECT
Take a picture of the items to be photographed, so you can refer to their scale, shapes, colours, and textures. Here, the subjects are handmade glass pendants.

② KEY WORDS
Write down the four or five words that best suggest the ethos of your brand – its mood, mission, and look.

③ MOOD
Look for images that convey the concept you are looking for. Here, the images and objects all suggest the tranquillity and timelessness of nature.

④ COLOURS
Pin up swatches in the colours of your subject, then add accent colours to find combinations that work for you.

⑤ LIGHT AND SHADOW
Lighting is a crucial mood-setter. Analyse how and why the lighting works in images that appeal to you.

⑥ BACKGROUND AND TEXTURE
Look for backdrops and textures that enhance your subject. Consider using contrast – for example, pairing smooth glass with rough wood or pottery.

⑦ FORM AND PATTERN
Think about shapes and patterns for props. For instance, jewellery can look stunning against props that are subtly reminiscent of a human form.

② # SEASCAPE
ORGANIC FORMS
OUTDOORS
NATURAL TEXTURES

③ This image sums up all the key words and forms the heart of the board

Layers of ancient rock convey a serene, ageless sense

#MOOD

Stripes echo a natural landscape, while the curved form suggests the human figure.

EDIT YOUR CHOICES

When you have finished collecting, it's time to edit. Look at each item again and reread your checklist. Discard everything that doesn't fit your brand and photography criteria. The more rigorous you are, the sharper and more relevant the moodboard will be.

8

#LIGHT
#SHADOW

5

Sharp shadow suggests strong sunlight, giving an outdoors feel

#FORM
#PATTERN

7

6

#BACKGROUND
#TEXTURE

FINAL IMAGE

4

#COLOURS

The coral fits in both colour and texture categories, so it sits between the two

THE RESULT

The moodboard led to the choice of distinctive stoneware vases as props. Their texture and colours suggest a beachscape's smooth, grey pebbles and blue horizon line, and their shape hints at a human form.

USE STOCK PHOTOGRAPHY

THE CASE FOR STOCK...

There are some pictures you simply can't take yourself. And even if you could, it's often cheaper and less complicated to source an existing photo. Stock photography is quick – you can instantly download an image and place it straight into your layout. Here are some situations in which stock imagery is a good bet.

SAVING MONEY

Setting up a professional photo session is not cheap. As well as a photographer, you might also need to pay for a studio, props, models, or a stylist. It's often cheaper to buy in what you need, especially if that's only one or two images.

PHOTOS OF PEOPLE

When you publish images of people, you usually need to obtain their permission, which can be tricky and time-consuming. Stock sources offer "model-released" images that have already been cleared for use, so you don't have to do any extra work.

SEASONS AND HISTORY

It isn't always the right time or place to get the picture you need. If it's the middle of summer and you want a snowscape, a stock image is the only solution. And if you need to show a scene from the past, you obviously have no choice but to look for an existing historical image.

Stock images are pictures that already exist, and which you can source and use, either free or for an agreed fee. They can add impact and variety to your designs, and often save you time and money, too.

This was shot with an extra-long telephoto lens, which is too expensive for most amateurs, and requires a high level of skill to operate

HARD-TO-TAKE IMAGES

Sometimes you simply can't position yourself where a professional photographer can, such as on a sporting starting line, up close to wildlife, or in a museum, where access is restricted.

... AND AGAINST

Stock is not always the best solution. Here are some of the pitfalls of using off-the-peg images in your work.

NON-EXCLUSIVITY

When you find your perfect image, the chances are that someone else has had the same thought. If a stock photo is a key element of your project, check that it hasn't already been used either by a competitor, or in a way that wouldn't reflect well on your project.

TOO GENERIC

Stock pictures, by their nature, have general appeal. You might find it difficult to source an image with enough specific meaning for your message or product.

VISUAL CLICHÉS

Unfortunately, many stock sources abound with trite, contrived images that can devalue your designs. Cheesy images such as "businessman on the beach with surfboard" should be avoided at all costs!

STOCK FACTS

If you're considering using third-party images, here is a run-down of essential information.

» **Free sources**
There are many sources for stock images, including some that are free – see page 210 for listings. Some pictures are free only for non-commercial use, so they can't be used to promote or sell anything. Other pictures are free if you both credit the photographer and leave the picture unaltered.

» **Try before you buy**
Most commercial sites have a free "comp" function, which means you can download and experiment with a low-resolution version before paying for the high-resolution file.

» **Credit the photographer**
Wherever possible, acknowledge the photographer – even if a credit is not a legal requirement, photographers always appreciate the courtesy.

» **Rights to use**
Commercial stock images are licensed as either "rights-managed" or "royalty-free". The former means you pay for one specific use only. The latter is for unlimited use, so is usually more expensive. For more on copyright law, see page 211.

» **Always seek permission**
If you want to use an image from any amateur sources that you come across, contact them first. Never use a picture if you haven't had written permission to do so.

HOW TO FIND US

Bay View is part of the charming Old Post Office, located in a quiet side street just a few minutes' walk from both Seatown's historic seafront and its lively commercial centre.

For prices and availability contact: adrienne@bayview.com

Bay View Apartment
Old Post Office
78 Bellair Road
Seatown ST10 1WY

TO MOTORWAY

Trinity Road
Station Avenue
Bellair Road
Beach Drive

1 Town Museum
2 Fisherman's church
3 Beach
4 Harbour
5 Shopping centre
6 Mount Park
7 Train station
8 Private car park

···· to the car park – 200m
···· to the train station – 400m
—— Motorway – 2km

AVAILABLE ALL YEAR

BAY VIEW
apartment

5-STAR RATING

MASTER BEDROOM ...floor has an ensuite ...entertainment ...balcony with ...views of the bay

SECOND BEDROOM is ideal for children, with twin beds, additional sofa bed, play area, and access to bathroom on the same floor

OPEN PLAN kitchen and living room lead to a secluded patio. Newly refurbished kitchen has a separate utility room.

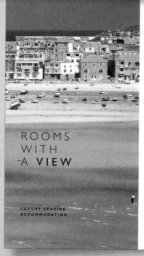

ROOMS
WITH
-A VIEW

LUXURY SEASIDE
ACCOMMODATION

FACILITIES /

2 bedrooms: 1 double bed 2 single beds | 1 bathroom | 1 ensuite shower room | Kitchen inc. gas hob, oven, and microwave | Dishwasher and washer-drier | TV with online and satellite channels | Free wifi | Garden and patio | Secure parking

⌃ THROUGH THE WINDOW

Taking its lead from the name of the apartment, this leaflet design creates a strong visual narrative that entices the reader inside. In the process, the selling point of the property's amazing views is conveyed well before you reach the core information.

FRONT COVER

INSIDE COVER AND
FACING PAGE

INSIDE SPREAD

OUTSIDE SPREAD

DESIGN A **TRI-FOLD LEAFLET**

Laid out over two spreads printed on either side of a single sheet, a tri-fold leaflet needs to be planned carefully so that the content makes sense and has impact, both when the leaflet is folded and when it is opened out in stages.

THE BRIEF

The owners of a recently refurbished holiday rental property would like to publicize their apartment to attract new bookings.

JOB SPEC:

- Overall aim: to design a folding leaflet for the apartment to give prospective guests practical information about the property. It should evoke a real sense of the pleasures of a seaside holiday.

- Convey relevant information:
WHAT is the property's name?
WHAT kind of property is it?
WHERE is it located?
WHO is it aimed at?
WHAT is its chief appeal?
HOW MANY people does it sleep?
WHAT facilities does it have?
HOW can it be booked?

- Highlight the newly decorated interior spaces of the property.

- Promote the property's location as a desirable holiday destination.

- Itemize the main facilities that renters will be able to use.

- Make the information as accessible as possible for a potentially international audience.

THE TOOLKIT

Your starting materials may only comprise a set of photographs, descriptive text, and lists of practical information. You can expand your toolkit with additional visual elements, such as symbols and maps. The main design here relies on the photography for colour, but you could also develop a colour palette for the leaflet. Factor in any existing brand identity, for example in a preferred set of fonts.

PHOTOGRAPHS

PHOTOS OF THE PROPERTY

PHOTOS OF THE AREA

ICONS

MAP

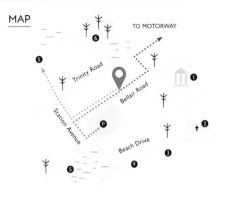

TYPEFACE AND FONTS

Gill Sans MT Pro Bold
Gill Sans MT Pro Medium
Gill Sans MT Pro Light

THE DESIGN PROCESS ≫

PLAN THE LAYOUT

Don't feel obliged to compartmentalize the design into stand-alone sections: consider how the content might work across two or more segments, particularly on the inside spread. Understanding how the leaflet opens out can suggest design strategies: the main design splits an image of the town across D and C segments so that the reader encounters an enticing view on first opening.

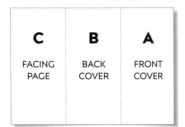

OUTSIDE

This guide shows how to arrange the segments and gives dimensions for an A4-sized sheet; a printer may also be able to provide a template for you to use.

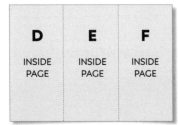

INSIDE

DIMENSIONS

A/D 100mm x 210mm
B/E 100mm x 210mm
C/F 97mm x 210mm

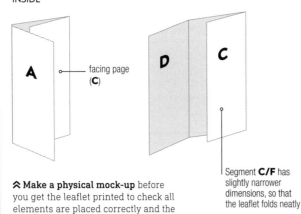

⌃ **Make a physical mock-up** before you get the leaflet printed to check all elements are placed correctly and the design works as a folded leaflet.

Segment **C/F** has slightly narrower dimensions, so that the leaflet folds neatly

» **CHOOSE YOUR FORMAT** – PAGE 128

VISUALIZE THE FACILITIES

Symbols and icons add an appealing illustrative dimension and convey information at a glance and to non-native speakers. Try creating your own, or search online for icons that can be downloaded and used for free.

CARTOON SOLID

CARTOON OUTLINE

REALISTIC SOLID

⌃ **Choose a set of icons** in keeping with the overall tone of the design. A quirky outline style works well with the light and characterful look aimed for. Solid icons may sit heavily on the page.

QUIRKY OUTLINE

VISUALIZE THE LOCATION

A map brings further visual appeal and utility to the leaflet. Download an existing open-source map, which would be free to use with the correct credit, or create your own. A homemade map adds charm and allows you to draft a layout that's tailored to your needs and omits irrelevant detail.

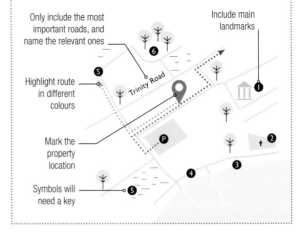

Only include the most important roads, and name the relevant ones

Include main landmarks

Highlight route in different colours

Mark the property location

Symbols will need a key

» ALTERNATIVE DESIGN

The main featured design sells the property through photographic content, which sings out from the pages. This alternative design draws on distinctive illustration to help imbue the property with an aspirational brand identity, which the reader can buy into.

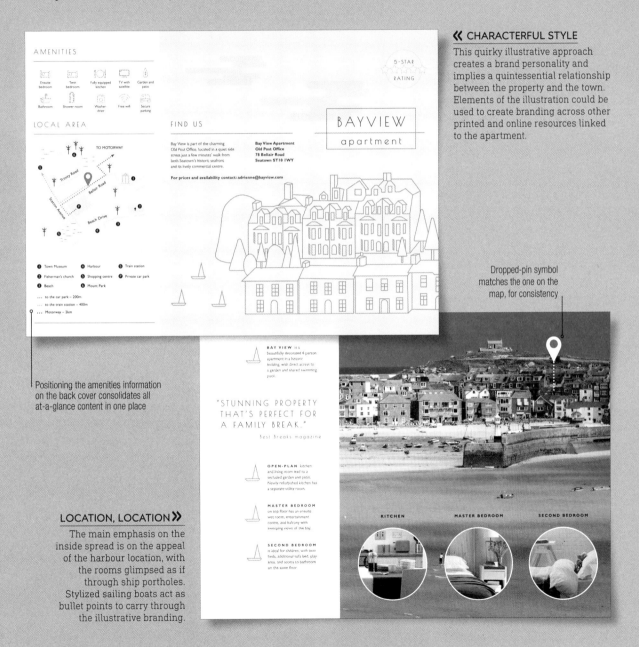

« CHARACTERFUL STYLE

This quirky illustrative approach creates a brand personality and implies a quintessential relationship between the property and the town. Elements of the illustration could be used to create branding across other printed and online resources linked to the apartment.

Dropped-pin symbol matches the one on the map, for consistency

Positioning the amenities information on the back cover consolidates all at-a-glance content in one place

LOCATION, LOCATION »

The main emphasis on the inside spread is on the appeal of the harbour location, with the rooms glimpsed as if through ship portholes. Stylized sailing boats act as bullet points to carry through the illustrative branding.

USING ILLUSTRATION IN DESIGN

WHY USE ILLUSTRATION?

Sometimes, illustration simply depicts a product or location. Or – and this is where it's really valuable – it can be a visual expression of a more abstract concept. And because it's bespoke to you, you can opt for the style that chimes with your own brand style to target a specific audience. Here are some of the ways in which illustration can work well for you.

The distinctive canal-side houses of Amsterdam are rendered in a sketchy, quirky style

Arrows and other devices can help to explain instructions visually

Black outlines create graphic shapes and bold, flat colours are child-friendly

REALITY WITH PERSONALITY

Illustration can depict something in a realistic enough way, while conveying a certain style – for instance, travel illustration allows the audience to see how a place looks and also get a sense of how it feels to be there.

SHOWING HOW

Illustration often allows you to show practical techniques more clearly than a photo can. You can simplify the information you are conveying by leaving out unnecessary detail, or making backgrounds less distracting.

TARGETING AN AUDIENCE

Because illustration is so adaptable, you can target a specific audience more easily than with photography. For instance, by using solid lines and blocks of primary colours, you can aim an illustration firmly at younger children.

Illustration is art for hire. It's not fine art, where often an artist's main motivation is self-expression; illustrators draw things that other people ask them for. Illustration can add individuality to your design work, enabling you to reach audiences in a way that photography often can't.

This cutaway imagines the behind-the-scenes hive of activity aboard a 15th-century sailing ship

A loose, pen-and-ink style is used to illustrate the Russian folk tale of Sadko the minstrel

Taken from a book on astrology, this montage of images illustrates text about navigating the "stormy waters" of a personal crisis

WHAT LIES BENEATH

Illustration is excellent for revealing things that can't be seen normally. Diagrams and cross-sections work by removing some elements of a 3D object, such as its outer covering, to show the internal features in context.

PREHISTORY AND FANTASY

Sometimes, photography is just not an option and illustration comes into its own – whether it's to depict real animals from prehistoric times, or visualizing characters from fiction, myth, or legend.

VISUALIZING AN IDEA

Illustration can be a subtle yet powerful medium for conveying complex or difficult ideas, whether it's an emotional state such as indecision, traits such as ambition, or concepts such as time or memory.

STYLES OF ILLUSTRATION

CHOOSING A STYLE

There are almost as many kinds of illustration as there are illustrators. Here is a checklist of factors to consider when selecting an illustration style:

» **Purpose**
What is your illustration for? The previous page showed just a few of the many roles illustration can play in a design: its purpose should have the biggest influence on the style you choose.

» **Brand**
Think about the mood, feel, and tone of voice of your brand or project. Is it youthful? Traditional? Sporty? Nostalgic? Choose a style that reflects your brand's personality.

» **Audience**
If you are targeting, for instance, older knitters, it's no good producing a set of Manga-style illustrations to decorate your website! If you have researched your audience, you should have a good idea of what they enjoy and expect. It can be good to challenge readers and viewers, but not to alienate them.

» **Medium**
Some styles are better suited to certain media than others. If your illustrations will mostly be viewed on a mobile device, for instance, you'll need a style that is bold enough to be visible at a small size and low resolution.

This flat, vector style of artwork suits matter-of-fact projects where attitude is unnecessary or undesirable, such as a manual or how-to guide.

A hand-drawn style, using descriptive scribbled and hatched strokes, is ideal for telling a story. The long, defined shadows imply a hint of menace.

Drawing is a supremely expressive and versatile medium for illustration. It can be as loose and expressive or as precise and detailed as you need it to be.

This pen-and-gouache style has life and immediacy. Bright colours and strong lines retain an eye-catching vibrancy even when viewed on the smallest screen.

If you are not planning to create your own artwork, you will need to find an illustrator for the job. Most have a preferred style or medium that they work in, so if you have a good idea of the kind of images you want, it will be easier to find and commission the ideal illustrator.

Loose lines and subtle, slightly faded colours suit fashion illustration perfectly, giving the feeling of the clothes' movement without too much detail.

Freehand digital software allows for very smooth transitions between colours or from light to dark, giving a soft, almost airbrushed quality to artwork.

This bold, blocky woodcut style has lots of personality. It can be used to evoke nostalgia, but is also useful for practical, how-to illustrations.

Smooth, black line around flat colour is a child-friendly style, but the solid colours also make it a suitable style for printing on fabric or other non-paper surfaces.

DIGITIZING ARTWORK

If illustrations are created in traditional media, such as paper, board, or canvas, they have to be digitized before they can be published, either in print or online. This can be done in one of two ways:

SCANNING

Scanning is the best way to digitize artwork. An ordinary home scanner is fine for smaller artworks – if you are planning to print, make sure you scan at the highest resolution. For bigger artworks, you'll need to use a large-format scanner: contact a print shop or specialist art-scanning company for prices.

PHOTOGRAPHING

Photographing artwork is quick and easy, but results can be variable, depending on the quality of your equipment and lighting. Always compare the photo to the original artwork as you will almost certainly need to correct the colour balance. You might have to use a professional photographer for especially large works or images in hard-to-photograph media such as oils, which can reflect light and create areas of glare.

Vale Farm

Chilli
INFUSED
EXTRA VIRGIN OLIVE OIL

INGREDIENTS: EXTRA VIRGIN OLIVE OIL, CHILLI

250 ML

Vale Farm

Garlic
INFUSED
EXTRA VIRGIN OLIVE OIL

INGREDIENTS: EXTRA VIRGIN OLIVE OIL, GARLIC

250 ML

Vale Farm

Rosemary
INFUSED
EXTRA VIRGIN OLIVE OIL

INGREDIENTS: EXTRA VIRGIN OLIVE OIL, ROSEMARY

250 ML

A GRAPHIC SLANT

These labels produce instant brand recognition with a design of two halves. The simple graphic device of a diagonal line divides the visual space in two, with a band of solid colour anchoring the product information. This bold use of colour is balanced by a contrastingly delicate, sketchy artwork style, which reflects the artisan qualities of the oils.

DESIGN A **RANGE OF LABELS**

Designing across a product range requires a careful balancing act: you must establish a strong and consistent brand identity, while at the same time enabling consumers to easily differentiate between products.

THE BRIEF

The brief is to design a suite of labels for a range of flavoured oils. The labels need to work individually and also as part of a recognizable range within the brand.

JOB SPEC:

- Overall aim: inspire consumers to choose your products and help them know what they are buying.

- Convey key information to the consumer:
  WHAT is the product name?
  WHICH company has manufactured the product?
  HOW MUCH of the product is contained within the package?
  HOW can people find out more about the company and products?

- Create a strong brand identity on the label, taking the company logo as the starting point.

- Text and visuals must be identifiable from a distance and the information easy to read.

- Label template must be applicable across the entire product range.

- The design must work within the physical parameters set by the dimensions of the packaging.

THE TOOLKIT

In addition to the company logo, the products themselves can be thought of as pre-existing design elements. Here, the infused flavours are an obvious source of inspiration for the visuals, directly informing the choice of illustrations and strongly influencing the colour palette. When selecting fonts, their significance for the tone of the branding is key, but also consider legibility and how they will work across the range.

COMPANY LOGO

Vale Farm

COLOUR PALETTE
BRAND COLOURS

CHILLI	GARLIC	ROSEMARY
C15 M85 Y100 K0	C10 M40 Y30 K0	C50 M20 Y60 K0

ARTWORKS

TYPEFACES AND FONTS

Clan Pro Thin

Clan Pro Narrow Book

Clan Pro Bold

Tartine Script Pro Bold

THE DESIGN PROCESS »

VISUALIZE THE INGREDIENTS

An image of the key flavour ingredient gives each product in the range its own identity. Artworks can add more personality than photos and will have a greater influence on brand identity.

WATERCOLOUR

Try out different artwork styles and gauge the moods they evoke so you can select the one that best reflects your brand.

VECTOR

PEN AND INK

《 STYLES OF ILLUSTRATION – SEE PAGE 110

(1)————————(2)————————(3)

FUTURE-PROOF YOUR PALETTE

This range contains three products, but in future the company may want to add more. Creating a larger colour palette now will give you options in reserve that you know work well within the range.

EXISTING RANGE

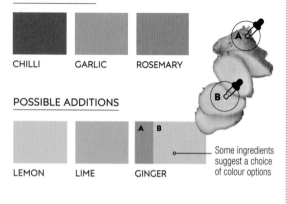

CHILLI   GARLIC   ROSEMARY

POSSIBLE ADDITIONS

LEMON   LIME   GINGER

Some ingredients suggest a choice of colour options

《 MAKE YOUR OWN COLOUR PALETTE – SEE PAGE 84

PLAN THE LAYOUT

Choose a bottle shape before you design labels as the shape will be a major factor in planning your label's size and layout. Many printers provide templates for you to work from. Work out the hierarchy of the label information so you can place the elements accordingly.

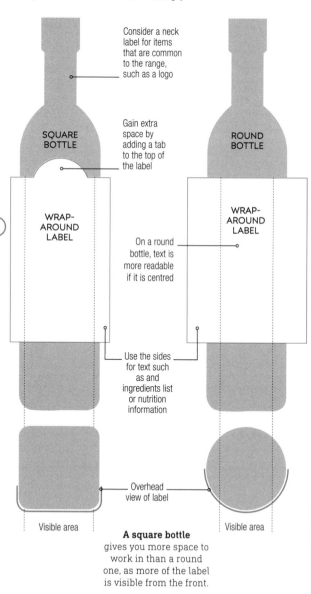

Consider a neck label for items that are common to the range, such as a logo

SQUARE BOTTLE

ROUND BOTTLE

Gain extra space by adding a tab to the top of the label

WRAP-AROUND LABEL

WRAP-AROUND LABEL

On a round bottle, text is more readable if it is centred

Use the sides for text such as and ingredients list or nutrition information

Overhead view of label

Visible area

Visible area

A square bottle gives you more space to work in than a round one, as more of the label is visible from the front.

⟫ ALTERNATIVES

For product packaging or labels, it can pay to devise a few different designs and conduct your own market research by testing them out on friends and customers. Find out which designs people connect with most and why: you need to understand their emotional reaction to see whether the design conveys the mood and feel you are aiming at.

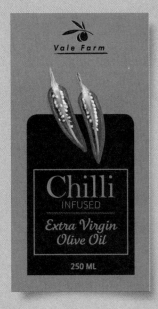

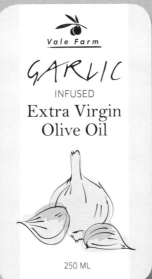

⟪ BOXED IN

Photos have a very different feel to artworks. This design allows the images to dominate by providing a backdrop of neutral charcoal-grey. Coloured type picks up the border colours: always make sure the text is readable against your chosen background.

⟪ HANDMADE STYLE

A sense of the craft involved in making the product is conveyed by loose, pen-and-wash artworks and a script font. White and pastels combined deliver visual impact and a distinctive brand identity.

TYPES OF DIGITAL ILLUSTRATION

VECTOR IMAGES

Vector images are built by joining points to form lines called paths. Paths can be straight or curved, and can connect to make complex shapes. The key feature of a vector image is that it can be used at any size with no loss of quality – the lines and shapes remain just as crisp.

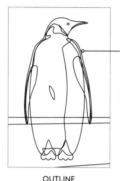

OUTLINE

Curves and lines are formed by joining points along paths

Paths can create closed shapes that are filled with colour

COLOUR APPLIED

RASTER IMAGES

Also known as bitmaps, these graphics are formed by millions of tiny coloured digital dots called pixels, arranged within a grid. This technology allows for very subtle gradations of colour and fine detail. Digital photos are also raster images, and any artwork that is scanned automatically becomes rasterized.

IMAGE AT 300DPI RESOLUTION

75DPI ENLARGEMENT

ANIMATION AND 3D IMAGES

3D imagery and animation used to be so expensive and time-consuming to create that it was beyond the reach of most – but the digital revolution has changed that. User-friendly software and powerful hardware make it easier to incorporate some animation into the most modest website, even if it's as minimal as a line appearing under a word, or a winking eye.

There is a vast range of software available to help you create digital art: as well as the well-known professional packages, there are plenty of free tools, too. You can use software either to mimic traditional styles and media, or to create unique digital artworks.

Vector programs tend to produce flat, 2D images, with minimal shading or contouring. Vectors are especially useful for logos and other graphic devices that need to be used at very different sizes.

Lines remain perfectly smooth when enlarged

ENLARGED IMAGE

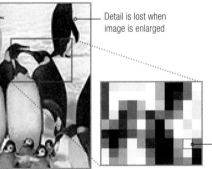

Detail is lost when image is enlarged

Every raster image has a fixed number of pixels (described as its resolution). This means that as you enlarge it, the pixels become more widely spaced, and the image loses detail. The greater the enlargement, the lower the resolution.

Each pixel is encoded to display a specific hue or tone

DETAIL OF PIXELS

3D illustrations involve creating the whole object using CAD (computer-aided design). The advantage of this is that you can portray the same object from many angles, without having to make a new image each time.

ROTATIONS OF SAME 3D IMAGE

DIGITAL FILE TYPES

Digital images can be created and saved in different digital formats, depending on their purpose and the medium in which they will be used.

VECTOR FORMATS

EPS These files are used to save a high-quality version of a graphic, suitable for high-resolution printing. EPS files aren't appropriate for online use and should first be converted to one of the raster formats below.

AI These files have been created and saved in the drawing application Adobe Illustrator. AI files are editable, so are most useful for work in progress that is being constantly amended.

PDF Essentially a snapshot of a digital image, page, or design, a PDF can be displayed on virtually any device or operating system. It is commonly used to send designs to a printer, or to display documents online. PDFs are not as easy to edit as some other formats, so are most useful when an illustration or design is final.

RASTER FORMATS

JPEG This file type is very versatile – JPEGs can have high enough resolution for printing, or be compressed for sending by email or for quick online uploads. All the image's data is compressed into one flat layer, so JPEGs are not as easy to edit as other formats.

TIFF TIFFs are image files that contain a large amount of data, meaning that images are high-resolution and rich in colour and detail. Excellent for printing, TIFFs are generally too large for most online uses.

PNG One of the most common formats for online use, PNG files are generally small and are good for retaining vibrant colours. Unlike JPEGs or TIFFs, a PNG image can have a transparent background, which is time-saving if you need a "cutout" effect.

PSD These files are created in the application Adobe Photoshop. They are multi-layered, making them fully editable – for instance, you can easily add shadows, effects, or textures to specific parts of an image. Files can become very large, so the format is mainly used during the creative stages of a project, then converted before printing or publishing online.

MAKE AN IMPACT WITH ILLUSTRATION

CHOOSE A STYLE – AND STICK TO IT

If you are using more than one illustration, it's usually best to stick to the same style, palette, and feel. Visual consistency sets the mood you are aiming for and helps the reader concentrate on the message. A recognizable style also helps people to identify you and your brand.

REPLACE WORDS WITH IMAGES

Graphic icons are used for everything from phone apps to showing how to assemble flat-pack furniture. Descriptive pictograms can do away with the need for text, make a design look sleek, and help you communicate with anyone in the world.

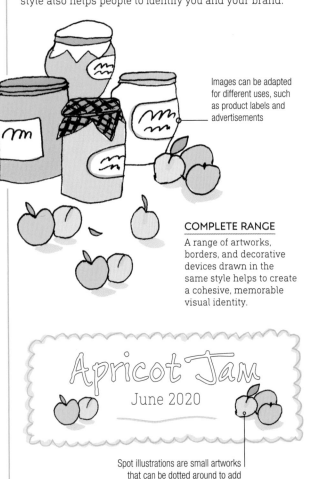

Images can be adapted for different uses, such as product labels and advertisements

COMPLETE RANGE

A range of artworks, borders, and decorative devices drawn in the same style helps to create a cohesive, memorable visual identity.

Apricot Jam
June 2020

Spot illustrations are small artworks that can be dotted around to add texture and interest

VISUAL INFORMATION

A map can be made virtually word-free by depicting locations, businesses, and public services with universally recognizable images.

What makes illustration so potent is that it's so personal – even the simplest line drawing is imbued with feeling and personality that's simply not present in a photo. Here are some ways that you can use those qualities to maximum effect.

SURPRISE THE AUDIENCE

Sometimes it seems as if photos are the only way to go – to illustrate recipes, perhaps, or show a range of products. But if everyone else in your sector is using photos and it all looks the same, consider illustration as a way to make your project unique.

SHOW OFF YOUR WARES

It can tricky to photograph food to show it in its best light. With illustrations, you won't have to worry that your cupcakes look too shiny or gooey.

USE CHARM AND WIT

It's often easier to inject wit or warmth with an illustration than with photos, or even text. Humour can be used to hook an audience, to personalize a message, or simply to make it more memorable.

VISUAL JOKES

A cartoon style means that your joke is more likely to transcend language or culture. But take care that the art chimes with your brand style, and remember – you'll be walking a fine line between fun and cheesiness.

IMAGE IN ALBUM COVERS

KARL KLEFISCH

1. DARING DIAGONALS

Designed by Karl Klefisch, Kraftwerk's 1978 album cover pays homage to the work of Russian Constructivist artist and designer, El Lissitzky, with strong diagonals created by the photo and the text, and the distinctive palette of white, red, and black.

RULE OF THIRDS

Buena Vista Social Club's eponymous album cover from 1997 shows Cuban musician Ibrahim Ferrer strolling down a street in Havana. Following the rule of thirds, the composition results in a balanced, dynamic image that leads the eye across the whole area.

3. POP ART PASTICHE

This 2009 album cover merges the hair from one photo of Madonna with her face from another. Splashes of hyper-saturated colour highlighting her hair, eyes, and lips are reminiscent of Andy Warhol's celebrated silkscreen prints of Marilyn Monroe.

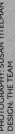

PHOTOGRAPHY: SUSAN TITELMAN
DESIGN: THE TEAM

MR. BRAINWASH

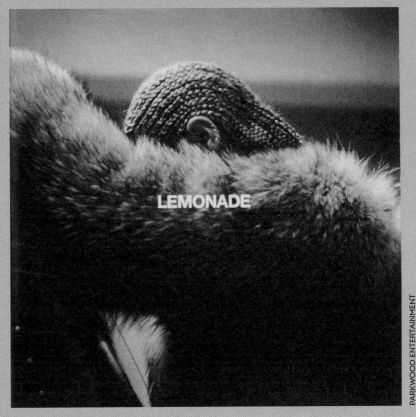

LEMONADE

PARKWOOD ENTERTAINMENT

BRIAN DUFFY

DAVID BOWIE

ALADDIN SANE

ALEX STEINWEISS

the voice of

FRANK SINATRA

orchestra under the direction of

COLUMBIA RECORDS

PETER BLAKE AND JANN HAWORTH

4. A STRIKE OF GENIUS

This simple, almost vulnerable portrait – shot by Brian Duffy for David Bowie's 1973 album *Aladdin Sane* – was made iconic by the vivid bolt of lightning across the musician's face. The red, blue, and white of the image are mirrored in the type, creating a sense of unity.

5. EMOTIVE IMAGERY

Though Beyoncé's face isn't visible, this tightly cropped and beautifully lit shot creates a strong sense of pathos, echoed by the simple, centred title. It's the perfect image for an album praised for its raw, honest explorations of heartbreak, rage, betrayal, and forgiveness.

6. CLASSIC COLLAGE

US record label Columbia Records were trailblazers in the field of cover art. In this 1946 album by Frank Sinatra, the collage-like design, combined with the colours, shapes, and fonts, is richly evocative of this era in America's design history.

7. CULTURAL STATEMENT

Surrounded by life-sized wax models and cutouts of notable people – including themselves – The Beatles take their place in this pantheon of fame. With this 1967 cover, artists Peter Blake and Jann Haworth created a bold and vibrant cover that is itself archetypal of pop culture

GORILLAZ

DEMON DAYS

JAMIE HEWLETT

8	9	10	11
	12	13	
		14	

8. SNAPSHOTS OF CHARACTER

Inspired by the cover art for The Beatles' 1970 album *Let It Be*, this 2005 album features mugshot-like caricatures of the four fictitious members of virtual band Gorillaz, as imagined by comic artist Jamie Hewlett.

9. CREATING INTRIGUE

Conceived by designer Storm Thorgerson, the cover of Pink Floyd's *Dark Side of the Moon* features no text – just a prism splitting light into colour on a black background. The clean, pared-back design piqued public interest and spawned a generation of imitations.

10. PLAYING WITH COLOUR

A 2002 compilation of The Rolling Stones' greatest hits, this artwork is a reworking of the band's famous "tongue and lip" logo, designed by John Pasche in 1970. Here, the colourway has been changed to blue and orange.

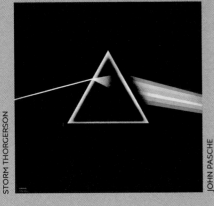

STORM THORGERSON

JOHN PASCHE

JAGEL & SLUTZKY GRAPHICS

ATLANTIC 1973

ANTHONY AUSGANG

GRAHAM LEWIS

DIVIDE

ADULT ART CLUB

11. EXPRESSIVE TYPE

For John Coltrane's classic 1961 album, US design team Jagel & Slutzky Graphics created an arresting, almost abstract image purely from type. The tightly compressed, "jumping" letterforms evoke Coltrane's famously rapid-fire cascading playing style,

12. SURREALISM

The cover artwork for MGMT's 2010 album *Congratulations* is by Anthony Ausgang, a US-based artist associated with the Lowbrow art movement. Bright colours and a perky style contrast jarringly with the darker subject matter of the illustration.

13. ABSTRACTION

Entirely devoid of text, the image on Wire's 1979 album *154* – a spare arrangement of coloured lines and curves – nonetheless succeeds in mirroring the music, which has been variously described as geometric, highly contoured, and minimalist.

14. VARIATIONS ON A THEME

This 2017 album was Ed Sheeran's third, the previous two being *Plus* and *Multiply*. Each uses a maths symbol for the main graphic. The design studio's brief was to create a natural, handmade feel, and to work on a theme of blue

PUTTING IT TOGETHER }

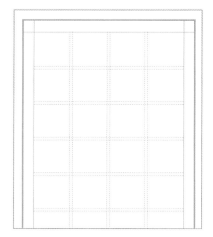

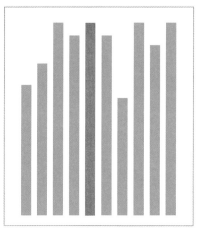

BASICS }

Once you have gathered together your visual elements, the next task is to combine them on a layout. The basics of choosing a format and of understanding the power of white space are fundamental to good design. And whether you are working on a simple layout or a more complex project, it's always helpful to focus your ideas and boost your creativity by making initial sketches. Now that you have a good understanding of the structures that underpin successful designs, you're all set.

CHOOSE YOUR FORMAT

PRINT FORMATS

Print remains a popular and fun way to be seen and noticed. Your audience may enjoy the sensory feel of tactile materials, and taking a break from spending time on screen – remember, of course, to use recyclable material. Successful print design maximizes the hands-on pleasure of using print, which digital can't provide.

PAPER FORMATS

Paper is a hugely versatile medium for design: it can be used in almost any shape or size, although it can be more cost-effective to use standard sizes if you are getting your designs printed professionally. Turn to page 208 for listings of standard paper sizes.

Landscape Also known as horizontal format, this shape is wider than it is tall. It's good for business cards, to fit long names or email addresses.

Portrait Also known as vertical format, this tall shape is popular for letters, text documents and posters.

FOLDING AND BINDING

Printed brochures and leaflets still have value as ways to promote project or businesses. They come in a variety of sizes and configurations.
The ways in which these printed materials are folded or bound together will influence your design choices.

DIGITAL FORMATS

Going online means you can potentially reach more people, quickly and cheaply. The main challenge of digital formats is that you have less control than with print over what the audience sees, because it depends so much on the device they use. Responsive design templates will resize across different formats (*see* page 175 for more on this), but you'll need to test your designs thoroughly to make sure they always look as you intended.

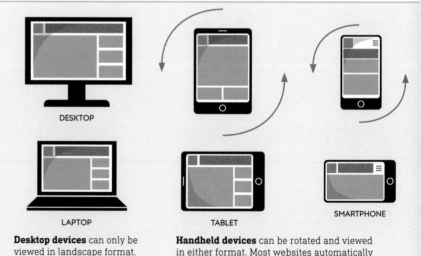

DESKTOP

LAPTOP

TABLET

SMARTPHONE

Desktop devices can only be viewed in landscape format.

Handheld devices can be rotated and viewed in either format. Most websites automatically rearrange content accordingly.

In design terms, format is the size, shape, and medium in which your design will be produced. Having a good sense of what you want to achieve and who you are targeting will help you to choose the right format for your design project.

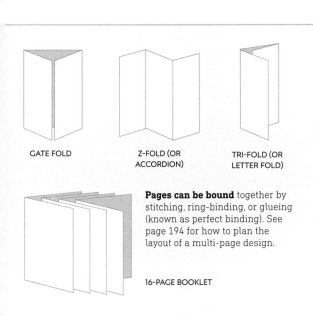

GATE FOLD

Z-FOLD (OR ACCORDION)

TRI-FOLD (OR LETTER FOLD)

Pages can be bound together by stitching, ring-binding, or glueing (known as perfect binding). See page 194 for how to plan the layout of a multi-page design.

16-PAGE BOOKLET

OTHER PRINT FORMATS

Printing doesn't just have to be on paper – there's a huge range of other media for your designs. Before you start, always ask your printer for advice on how to set up your layouts for the best results.

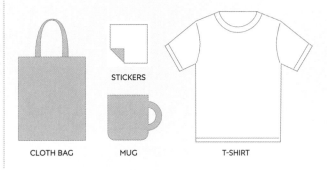

STICKERS

CLOTH BAG

MUG

T-SHIRT

SOCIAL MEDIA FORMATS

The social media arena is fast-changing and this is a challenge for you as a designer. Every platform has its own specifications for image size (measured in pixels), format, and type. You'll have to alter designs for each platform so that they are not cropped or distorted. Here are some common formats for social media, but always check current guidelines!

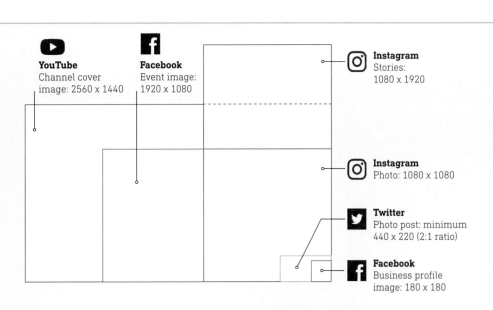

YouTube
Channel cover image: 2560 x 1440

Facebook
Event image: 1920 x 1080

Instagram
Stories: 1080 x 1920

Instagram
Photo: 1080 x 1080

Twitter
Photo post: minimum 440 x 220 (2:1 ratio)

Facebook
Business profile image: 180 x 180

USING WHITE SPACE

WHITE SPACE BASICS

On a typical layout, there are two kinds of white space: the tiny spaces that occur within text, and the larger spaces designed to frame and separate different elements. Both are important factors in the success of your designs.

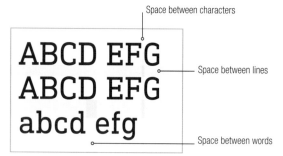

Space between characters

Space between lines

Space between words

SMALL SPACE

The gaps between letterforms, words, and lines of text are known as micro space, and are adjusted to make text more readable and attractive. For more about handling space within text, **see** page 54, Measuring type.

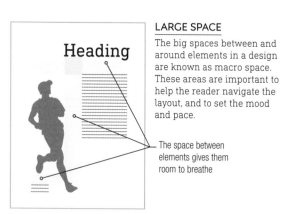

Heading

LARGE SPACE

The big spaces between and around elements in a design are known as macro space. These areas are important to help the reader navigate the layout, and to set the mood and pace.

The space between elements gives them room to breathe

SPACE AND LAYOUTS

MARGINS

The size of a margin – the space between the design elements and the edge of the layout – is a key factor in how a page works. Narrow margins tend to make a layout look crowded, while wider margins convey a sense of organization, and allow the viewer to focus on the subject.

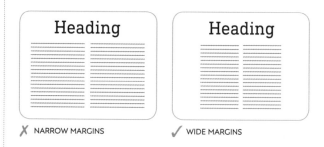

Heading   Heading

✗ NARROW MARGINS   ✓ WIDE MARGINS

SPACE AFFECTS PACE

The space between elements on the page affects the legibility of your design. It affects the total communication, both pictures and text. If you are designing for a small format like a phone, keep it simple and use one column.

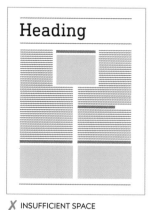

Heading

Heading

✗ INSUFFICIENT SPACE   ✓ BETTER USE OF SPACE

White space doesn't have to be white – the term refers to the room that is deliberately left within blocks of text, between elements, or around the margins of a page. Master the use of space and your designs will both look more professional and work better.

LESS IS MORE

White space can make a powerful statement, exuding confidence and authority. It is often associated with luxury – think of the way some high-end restaurants present food arranged at the centre of a huge, white plate. The website below takes full advantage of space to create a cool, uncluttered, but still hard-working design.

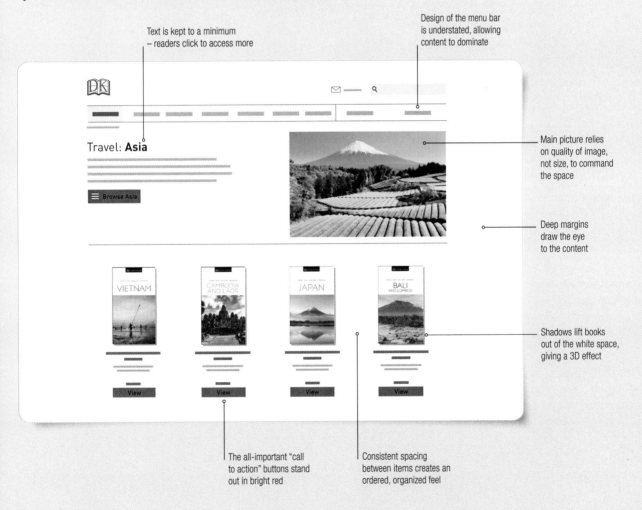

Text is kept to a minimum – readers click to access more

Design of the menu bar is understated, allowing content to dominate

Travel: **Asia**

Browse Asia

Main picture relies on quality of image, not size, to command the space

Deep margins draw the eye to the content

VIETNAM

CAMBODIA AND LAOS

JAPAN

BALI AND LOMBOK

View   View   View   View

Shadows lift books out of the white space, giving a 3D effect

The all-important "call to action" buttons stand out in bright red

Consistent spacing between items creates an ordered, organized feel

STRUCTURING A LAYOUT

GOLDEN RATIO

The Ancient Greeks were the first to notice that a certain proportion, often seen in nature, could be applied to art and architecture to create pleasing and balanced designs. Based on a mathematical equation, the ratio has been explored by scientists and artists including Fibonacci and Leonardo da Vinci.

The basis of the golden ratio is the golden rectangle. Its sides have a ratio of 1:1.6, which means that if the short sides are 1cm long, the long sides will measure 1.6cm.

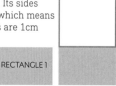

RECTANGLE 1

RECTANGLE 2

1. Start with a rectangle of 1cm x 1.6cm.

2. The next rectangle is made by drawing a square with sides the same length as the long sides of rectangle 1.

3. Make progressively bigger rectangles by adding squares on the long side of the last rectangle.

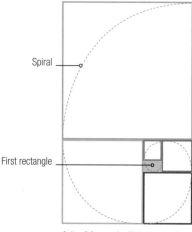

Spiral

First rectangle

A "golden spiral" is created by the rectangles. This shape is often seen in nature – for instance, on a snail's shell.

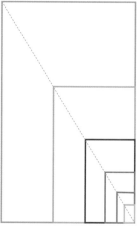

The rectangles created are all in the same proportion, which is why designs based on the pattern look so pleasing.

USING THE GOLDEN RATIO

The golden ratio can help you to size and position elements. You don't even have to draw it yourself: there are plenty of apps available that perform calculations so you can set up your working space to the right proportions, and others that overlay the golden spiral onto your photos or designs.

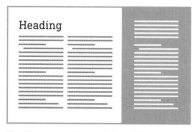

Heading

Use the proportions of the golden ratio to divide a web page into a main section and sidebar.

The golden spiral is useful for cropping images. The spiral's centre is the place to which the eye is most drawn. Positioning the dog's face there gives the image an appealing focal point.

No matter how simple the design, it needs structure – an ordered and logical way of positioning elements. There are many ways to build a layout, but the aim is the same – to convey the message as meaningfully and attractively as possible. Here are three of the best and most common structures.

RULE OF THIRDS

The rule of thirds is based on the premise that a space divided into three feels more comfortable and looks more pleasing than one split in half. A space is divided horizontally and vertically, creating a grid of nine rectangles. The lines and intersection points then provide a guide when positioning elements.

USING THE RULE OF THIRDS

Using a grid shows you the "sweet spots" in a layout – the points at which the horizontal and vertical lines intersect. Place the most important elements on these points to maximize their visual impact in your layout. There may be times when breaking the rules works best.

LAYOUT DIVIDED INTO NINE SECTIONS

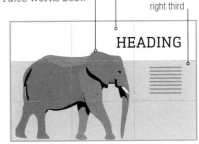

Image sits in the bottom two-thirds of the grid

Heading is placed in the top third

Text sits in right third

LAYOUT BASED ON RULE OF THIRDS

MODULAR STRUCTURES

In modular designs, the whole space is divided into blocks of the same size – these can be square or rectangular. Having more blocks (or modules) allows more flexibility than using a simple "rule of thirds" structure. For more on creating a modular grid, see page 158.

USING MODULAR LAYOUTS

A modular layout can be as simple or complex as you need. The risk is that everything can look square and samey. Varying the scale, leaving white space, and using cut-out images will all help to change the pace.

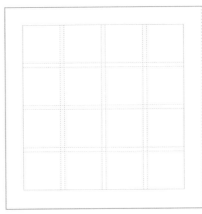

LAYOUT DIVIDED INTO EQUAL MODULES

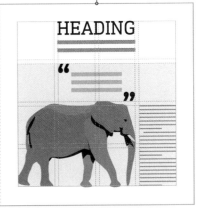

Structure allows for a variety of shapes and sizes of images and text

LAYOUT BASED ON MODULAR STRUCTURE

SKETCH OUT YOUR LAYOUTS

THE PROCESS

This step-by-step process is a good way to approach visuals. It doesn't matter if your drawing skills are limited – the act of making the sketches is as valuable a part of the process as the finished drawings. Visualization is a tool to focus your ideas, and to quickly show others what you are thinking, and the process is equally valuable for print and digital design.

STEP 1
BRAINSTORM

Start by jotting down any words that describe how you want to approach your project. You may already have key words relating to your project (*see* page 32, Draft your verbal brand) – if so, refresh your memory by looking back through them.

STEP 2
COMPILE A BRIEF

Write a summary of your aims. If you have prepared a project brief (*see* page 15) and have worked on your brand, refer to these at this point. List all the elements to be included, such as text, images, and logos.

FROM SKETCH TO LAYOUT

The brief in this example is to create a set of cards to accompany a book on astrology. Each sign of the zodiac has a separate card, setting out the essential facts. This sequence shows the process of designing the front of the card for sun sign Leo.

Initial sketches are based on these key words: lion; fire sign; king of the jungle; constellation; symbol, sun

Ideas are worked into rough sketches of possible layouts

RAPID SKETCHES

WORKING UP IDEAS

Making preparatory sketches and roughs is an essential stage in producing layouts. Rather than diving straight on to the computer, spend time thinking about the brief and trying out ideas on paper. This way, you'll almost certainly come up with better, more creative ways to achieve your design aims.

STEP 3
START SKETCHING

Make rough sketches to explore any ideas that the keywords and brief inspire. Work quickly – consider allowing yourself a maximum of 30 seconds before moving on. The aim is to loosen up your thoughts and get your creativity flowing.

STEP 4
WORK UP IDEAS

Take the ideas you like best and work them into more detailed visuals, based on the format of the layout. If you prefer, you can use the computer for this stage, but try to keep your thoughts and design ideas fluid.

The final design includes visual representations of the key words that describe Leo

LEO
23 JULY–22 AUGUST

Warm, bright, and charismatic, Leo is a regal sign, but full of fun too. Leos possess dignity, self-confidence, and a sense of style along with a generous nature.

FINISHED LAYOUT

A more finished sketch shows how images and text would work together

FINAL SKETCH

FREE
ENTRY

COMPLIMENTARY PASTRY
WITH EVERY COFFEE

LIVE
MUSIC

AND MORE!

GREEN PARK BEANS

INVITATION

GRAND OPENING

7 AUGUST
10:00 – 12:00

GREEN
PARK
BEANS

85 PARK STREET, BROOKFIELD, BF19 1XW

READ ME!
This design takes the direct route to delivering its message – the word "INVITATION" dominates. Filling the text with the coffee-bean pattern helps to unify the two halves of the layout. The exaggerated size and accent colour of the number 7 adds a graphic element.

DESIGN AN **EVENT FLYER**

A flyer must work quickly to draw the reader's eye, deliver information, and call the reader to action. In this project, the aim is simple – to inspire people to attend the opening of a new coffee shop.

THE BRIEF

A flyer is an excellent way to spread a message to lots of people in a specific geographical area. This flyer is advertising a local coffee shop opening, so it needs to communicate the key event details succinctly and in an eye-catching design.

JOB SPEC:

- Overall aim: to publicize the opening of a new coffee shop.
- Design print material (flyer) to promote the event.
- Convey all the relevant information in a direct, appealing way:
  WHO is it about?
  WHAT is happening?
  WHERE is the event?
  WHEN is it happening?
  WHY should I attend – what's in it for me?
- Stay within the brand identity, and make a visual connection between the flyer and any existing material, such as menus or interior decor. If the brand identity is friendly and relaxed, the flyer should reflect this.

THE TOOLKIT

Your design toolkit is made up of the must-have elements that form the essential look of your brand. This can include a logo, the colour palette, and standard fonts.

For specific design projects, you might want to add optional colours and other design elements to the basic toolkit, but be careful not to dilute or confuse the brand message. Here, the designer decided to keep it simple, using only elements already in the coffee shop's brand style guide.

DESIGN ELEMENTS

COFFEE BEAN PATTERN

COMPANY LOGO

COLOUR PALETTE

BRAND COLOURS

COFFEE	TEAL	PINK
C0 M40 Y25 K25	C75 M5 Y30 K0	C0 M80 Y20 K0

STANDARD COLOURS

BLACK	WHITE
C0 M0 Y0 K100	C0 M0 Y0 K0

TYPEFACE AND FONTS

Avenir Next LT Pro Condensed Heavy

Avenir Next LT Pro Condensed Bold

Avenir Next LT Pro Condensed Demi

Avenir Next LT Pro Condensed Medium

Avenir Next LT Pro Bold

Avenir Next LT Pro Regular

THE DESIGN PROCESS »

DECIDE ON THE MESSAGE

The golden rule is to keep your text to a minimum. The more concise you are, the more powerful the visual message. Write down only the essential information:

Flyer's purpose: Invitation

Company: Green Park Beans

Event: Opening of new café

Venue: 85 Park Street, Brookfield, BF19 1XW

Date and time: 7 August from 10am–12pm

Additional information: Free entry; complimentary pastry with every coffee; live music and more!

THINK ABOUT COLOURS

Your design should have visual impact, but not at the expense of readability. Try out combinations to ensure that text will show against the background.

The teal/brown combination provides a pop of bright colour but is still easy to read

« HOW COLOURS INTERACT – SEE PAGE 78

TRY OUT SOME VISUALS

Most designers find it helpful to sketch out rough layouts before designing on the computer. Refer to your ranking of the text as you work, always ensuring the main message is clear.

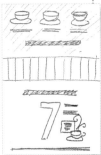

Don't spend long on your initial sketches. Use simple lines and shapes to indicate size and position of text and graphics.

---

① ② ③ ④ ⑤

RANK THE TEXT

Decide the relative importance of each piece of text, then use different sizes and weights of type to indicate this.

> ② **GREEN PARK BEANS**
> ① # INVITATION
> ③ **GRAND OPENING**
> ⑤ FREE ENTRY; COMPLIMENTARY PASTRY WITH EVERY COFFEE; LIVE MUSIC AND MORE!
> ④ **7 AUGUST** 10AM-12PM
> ⑥ 85 Park Street, Brookfield, BF19 1XW

1. The word "invitation" is the main focus of the layout
2. The company name is next in importance
3. The event description ranks third
4. The event's date and time should be prominent
5. The benefits of attending will entice readers
6. The venue address is small, but still easily readable

« TYPE HIERARCHY – SEE PAGE 142

CHOOSE A FORMAT

Is your flyer going to be **printed**, **digital**, or **both**? Printed flyers are easy to distribute – simply hand them out to the public. This design is for an A5-sized printed flyer: conveniently small, but large enough to have visual impact.

A5 LANDSCAPE
210MM x 148MM

A5 PORTRAIT
148MM x 210MM

Make your sketches the same size or to the same proportions as your chosen format. That way, you'll ensure that the elements will fit together on your layout.

Be bold at this stage and try out different ideas. Rejected designs help you to focus on the strategies that do work.

ALTERNATIVE DESIGNS

The best thing about design can also be one of its biggest challenges – there's never only one route to a successful result. Here are three equally impactful ways to assemble the flyer, each delivering bags of visual punch using only the brand's standard elements.

« COOL AND COLOURFUL

This confident design deconstructs the elements – even the logo – and puts them back together in unexpected ways. The result is both witty and sophisticated, with a nod to classic Bauhaus designs of the 1930s.

« CENTRE OF ATTENTION

In this rather friendly, welcoming design, the cup from the logo, repeated and enlarged, is the star. The text is centred, with emphasis created by the contrasting weights of type.

« TURN IT AROUND

A flyer's orientation (whether it is portrait- or landscape-format) has a major influence on the feel of the design. Here, the horizontal format allows room for space around the text, creating a relaxed, uncluttered mood.

HIERARCHY }

The graphic designer's role is to take a jumble of information and organize it so that it's easy to understand. Hierarchy – showing the relative importance of different elements – plays a key role in achieving that goal. By smart handling of typography and colour, and by manipulating the size and scale of different elements, you can create order. You can lead your audience easily to the message – and, crucially, make that journey fun, enjoyable, and beautiful.

USE TYPOGRAPHY TO CREATE ORDER

RANKING TEXT

The designer needs to present information so that readers understand the order in which to read – from most to least important. Many factors affect how a piece of text can dominate, including size, colour, and the type's position in relation both to other text and the white space around it. It is important that, when you style different kinds of text, you not only treat them in ways that reflect their importance, but keep in mind that the different styles need to work together as part of the whole design.

Before you start styling text, decide on the hierarchy. List the different kinds of text in your design, then rank each category in order of its importance. Most layouts have at least three levels of text, but complex ones can have more.

Level 1

The highest level is used only for the most important text: usually a heading or title.

Level 2

This covers the next rank down and could include subheadings and introductions. It needs to catch the eye and tempt an audience to read the main text.

Level 3

This is the text that makes up most of your layout – the body copy. It needs to be small enough to fit in all the information but easy to read in longer blocks.

WAYS TO ACHIEVE HIERARCHY

There are many options for creating typographical order – use these methods singly or in combination for lively, readable layouts that are both inviting and easy to follow.

① SIZE

An obvious way to show that information is important is to make it big on the page or screen – the larger the type, the more it commands attention. This method works best in layouts where there is plenty of space, such as a large-format poster or newspaper pages.

② UPPERCASE

Uppercase characters attract attention and flag up key information. They are most useful for short headings and phrases, as they can be hard to read in longer chunks, and a lot of uppercase characters will look "shouty".

③ WEIGHT

You can use a heavier font to signal text that is more important than the regular type. You are literally giving more weight to the text, and the viewer's eye will be drawn to it.

④ POSITION

Readers naturally look at a page from top to bottom, making the top of a layout the conventional location for headings. But depending on the structure of your layout, there will be other, equally eye-catching positions for key text: see pages 132–133 for more on layout structures.

⑤ COLOUR

Colours attract the eye, so can be used to direct the viewer towards high-ranking text. Use coloured text sparingly: too much diminishes impact and it can be hard to read. Colour is useful where space is tight, such as on smartphones.

⑥ CONTRAST

Using different typefaces to fulfil different roles in your layout can make a design more interesting. Many display fonts are specifically designed to convey personality, and will naturally draw the eye within a design.

As a designer, your aim is to help the audience to navigate a layout – and the way you use and organize type will be crucial to your success. Here's how to set out type so that readers know where to start and finish, and can easily find the information they are looking for.

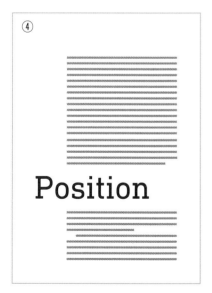

USE COLOUR TO CREATE ORDER

BLOCKS OF COLOUR

Setting sections of text in a coloured background is an effective way to separate and organize information. This can also be used to flag up the same kind of text across several pages. Make sure type is legible against your chosen colour.

REPETITION

Repeating a graphic element in the same colour helps to draw the viewer's eye through a layout and is a useful way to organize long text into more manageable sections.

Banner

A strip behind a heading is known as a banner.

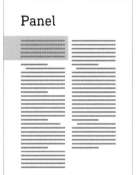

Panel

The introduction paragraph is highlighted with a coloured panel.

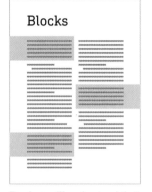

Blocks

Readers will understand that the three coloured panels are related in some way.

Bars

Coloured bars divide the layout into three distinct sections.

Pull-out

The eye is drawn to a quotation that has been pulled out of the text.

Strip

A vertical strip separates two stories on the same page.

Numerals

The numbers are easy to pick out, and indicate the path through the text.

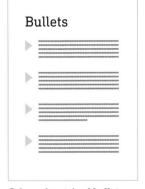

Bullets

Coloured, outsized bullets clearly mark the text's four different sections.

Colour is another tool a designer can use to organize information, highlighting important elements and guiding the eye through more complex layouts. The previous page showed how coloured type can be used – here are other ways colour can help to achieve order and cohesion.

CONTRAST

The eye is naturally drawn to the brightest colours, so use them to pick out the most important visual information. This is especially effective when the rest of the colour palette is understated.

Contrasting colours make it easy to identify different kinds of text.

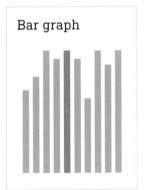

The key data on this infographic can be picked out instantly by the viewer.

The "buy" button is usually the most eye-catching element on a shop's page.

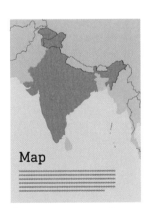

On a map, use contrasting colour to pinpoint a region or country within a larger area.

COLOUR CODING

Assigning a specific, consistent meaning to a colour can be useful when organizing more complex information, for instance on a railway map showing different lines. You can also use this method to help an audience navigate the different sections of a website.

Colour can be used to identify different categories, as with these recycling bins.

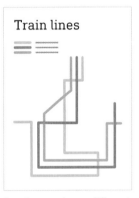

On a transport map, different lines are coded for easy route planning.

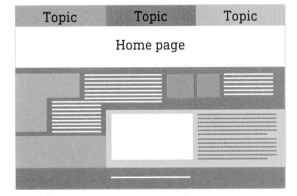

A website homepage uses colour to link its lead stories of the day to the different areas of interest on the site.

USE SCALE TO CREATE ORDER

SIZE AND SCALE

These terms are often used interchangeably, but they are slightly different, and both are crucial factors in creating designs that work.

SIZE

In graphic design terms, size is a fixed value – for instance, a paragraph of text can be set at a size of 12PT. Designers select the appropriate point size to ensure that text will be readable in whatever format or medium they are working.

SCALE

Scale also describes something's size – but in terms of its relationship to elements around it. An audience will usually look at the biggest element first, so getting scale right is crucial to convey effectively the key part of your message.

In each example, the first word is the same size

size   scale

size   scale

In the first example, the word "size" is larger than "scale" and comes before it – the viewer would definitely read it first. In the second graphic, the word "scale" dominates and the eye is drawn to it, even though the natural place to start reading is usually on the left.

The scale of the second word makes the first look small by comparison

WAYS TO USE SCALE

As well as indicating importance, scale can bring drama or wit to a design. The scale of type is important, as discussed on page 142. Here are some other aspects of scale to consider when organizing a layout.

SCALING LETTERS

Upscaling the first letter of a paragraph creates a drop cap (short for "dropped capital"). The character extends below the baseline, taking up two or more lines of space. A drop cap can add a graphic element to text, while making it clear where the reader should begin reading.

DROP CAP EXTENDED OVER THREE LINES

DROP CAP EXTENDED OVER FIVE LINES

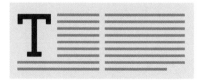

DROP CAP EXTENDED OVER SEVEN LINES

The bigger something is, the more attention it gets. But size is also relative – something can appear big or small, depending on its surroundings and relationship to other elements. Skilful handling of size and scale is key to creating order and balance in your layouts.

ZOOM OUT, ZOOM IN

Space can give a sense of scale to a design. Text or images set within a larger area of white space will draw the eye and make an impact. Conversely, you can also attract attention by making an element appear to be too big for the space it occupies.

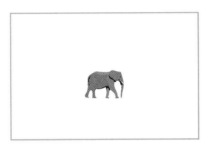

Surrounded by space, an image commands attention, however small.

By making it seem almost too big for its frame, the elephant's size is emphasized.

USING BLEED

Bleed is the term used when an image extends beyond the boundaries of a layout. Using bleeds can emphasize the scale of an image or its subject. As long as you show enough of the subject, the viewer's brain will "add in" the missing visual information so that it still gets the sense of the whole elephant.

The image sits within the frame. Viewers make an assumption about the elephant's size based on real-life knowledge.

By showing only its front half, the scale can be increased to give a more vivid impression of size.

LIFE-SIZE – OR NOT

You can inject a sense of drama or playfulness by scaling elements in a surprising way. Making things comparatively smaller or larger than in reality can completely change the meaning of your visual message.

Man and elephant are shown at a realistic scale: the image conveys factual information about their relative sizes.

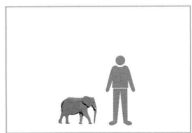

By adjusting the scale, the designer may now be suggesting a different, more nuanced message.

JUNE **07** 2021

...th their families

...IE &

...CUS

...ate their marriage

...ouse Hotel
...Square
...n TL9 1AB
...begin at 4pm

...ANCING IN THE
...TO FOLLOW

...@internet.net
...wning Road,
...ough
...AG

ELEGANT AND APPROACHABLE

The front of this fold-out design turns the date of the wedding into a striking graphic feature. The numerals, cut from smooth, thick card, vividly stand out on the rich burgundy backdrop. The little snapshot and message on the back adds an intimate, personal angle that softens the formality of the occasion.

SEE YOU SOON!

FRONT WHEN CLOSED

BACK WHEN CLOSED

JUNE **07** 2021
Together with their families

**ROSIE &
MARCUS**

invite you to celebrate their marriage

Woodley House Hotel
Gordon Square
Tilborough TL9 1AB
The service will begin at 4pm

**DINNER AND DANCING IN THE
GREAT BARN TO FOLLOW**

RSVP: rsharp@internet.net
or to: 23 Browning Road,
Tilborough
TL1 5AG

FRONT OF CARD

SEE YOU SOON!

BACK OF CARD

DESIGN AN **INVITATION**

A big celebration is the ideal opportunity to make the most of what print design can offer. A beautifully designed invitation on luxurious paper or card feels very special – a fitting way to show guests how much you value them.

THE BRIEF

A couple planning their wedding require an invitation to the ceremony, to mail out to 100 guests. They want the invitation to reflect the visual theme that they have already chosen.

JOB SPEC:

- Overall aim: to design and print a wedding invitation that will both set out practical information and look special enough to convey the significance of the occasion.

- Convey the essential information:
WHAT is the occasion?
WHEN is it happening?
WHERE is it being held?
HOW do invitees respond?

- To work, alongside the printer and within the set budget, to decide on format and size, plus any features such as die-cutting or special inks.

- Follow the theme, colour palette, and visual style that has already been set for the wedding day.

THE TOOLKIT

A large-scale event often follows a visual theme, co-ordinating elements such as outfits, table settings, flowers, and printed materials. The loose theme of this wedding is a take on Art Nouveau, an elegant and sophisticated decorative style popular in the early 20th century, and the invitation will reflect this. The couple are also keen to include a personal, informal message to friends and family.

PHOTOS

PHOTO OF THE COUPLE

MOODBOARD

DESIGN AND COLOUR INSPIRATION BOARD

COLOUR PALETTE

This invitation will be printed using a special ink called a spot colour. This enables you to match a specific shade more closely than by standard, four-colour printing.

BLACK
C0 M0 Y0 K100

BURGUNDY
PANTONE 506

WHITE
PAPER COLOUR

TYPEFACES

The main typeface, Willow, is a modern digital font, inspired by the work of architect Charles Rennie Mackintosh. It takes its name from a sign Mackintosh designed for the Willow Tea Rooms in Glasgow, Scotland, in 1903.

WILLOW STD REGULAR
ITC Avant Garde Gothic

THE DESIGN PROCESS »

PLAN THE LAYOUT

The invitation's format is known as Z-fold (or accordion-fold). This uses two parallel creases to create six panels of equal size – three on each side of the sheet. The folds are made in opposite directions, so that the finished shape looks like the letter "z".

CREATING A Z-FOLD

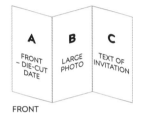

A	B	C
FRONT – DIE-CUT DATE	LARGE PHOTO	TEXT OF INVITATION

FRONT

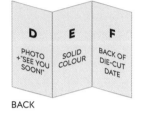

D	E	F
PHOTO + "SEE YOU SOON!"	SOLID COLOUR	BACK OF DIE-CUT DATE

BACK

Dimensions Size of each panel: 99 x 175mm (3.9 x 6.9in). Your printer will advise you on cost-effective sizes.

THINK ABOUT COLOUR

Using a special ink for the invitation is more expensive than standard printing, but the colour will be more vibrant and consistent. Pantone is a colour-matching system used in many industries, so once you decide on a shade, you could use it to colour everything from bridesmaids' dresses to the wedding cake!

Pantone colour matching was used to pick an ink the same colour as the peony

BURGUNDY
PANTONE 506

DUOTONE IMAGE
The original colour image was converted to greyscale, then printed using the chosen ink.

DECIDE ON SPECIAL FEATURES

An effective way to add interest to square or rectangular formats is to cut shapes into the paper or card. This is known as die cutting (if using a manually operated cutter), or laser cutting (using an automated laser technique). The technique can be used to create a huge variety of effects – the only limit is the designer's imagination and budget. For this design, the designer cut the numbers of the wedding date out to show the coloured card on the layer beneath.

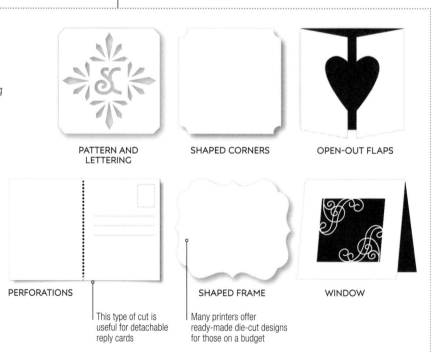

PATTERN AND LETTERING

SHAPED CORNERS

OPEN-OUT FLAPS

PERFORATIONS

This type of cut is useful for detachable reply cards

SHAPED FRAME

Many printers offer ready-made die-cut designs for those on a budget

WINDOW

» **PAPER WEIGHTS AND FINISHES**
– SEE PAGE 206–207

ALTERNATIVE DESIGNS

An invitation is a perfect opportunity for the hosts to set the tone for the occasion. Whether it's a glorious, grand-scale spectacle or a low-key, intimate celebration, the right design can perfectly convey a theme or style, anticipating the day to come. As with all design, the key is to have a clear idea of the outcome you want before you start to make decisions.

Rosie & Marcus

We'd love you to join us to celebrate our wedding

07 June 2021
Wedding at 4pm – dancing from 7 till late!

Woodley House Hotel
Gordon Square
Tillborough
TL9 1AB

RSVP: rsharp@internet.net
or: 23 Browning Road,
Tillborough
TL1 5AG

JUNE **07** 2021

Together with their families

ROSIE & MARCUS

Invite you to celebrate their marriage

Woodley House Hotel
Gordon Square
Tillborough
TL9 1AB

DINNER AND DANCING IN THE GREAT BARN TO FOLLOW

RSVP: rsharp@internet.net;
23 Browning Road,
Tillborough
TL1 5AG

Listen up!

⌃ TEXTURE AND SHIMMER

A combination of thick, textured card and understated gold-foil detailing gives this single-page design a classy finish. Proof that you don't need to spend a fortune on special print effects for a memorable, classic result.

⌃ INTIMATE AND INFORMAL

This design is a contrast to the others, taking the candid photo of the couple as its inspiration. The "instant-photo" styling, casual script font, and informal language are all in keeping with the playful, spontaneous mood of the central image – all of which fits with the couple's plans for the wedding day itself.

COMPOSITION IN BOOK COVERS

ADALIS MARTINEZ

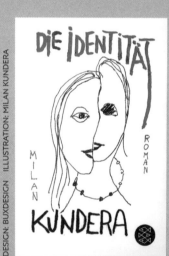

DESIGN: BUXDESIGN   ILLUSTRATION: MILAN KUNDERA

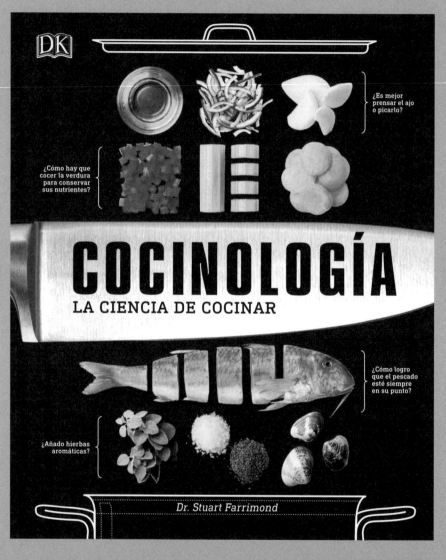

1. STRIKING SIMPLICITY

For the German edition of this 2016 novel about a Jewish survivor of WWII, designer Adalis Martinez used a block-printed image of matches. The result is simple but symbolic, suggesting both transience and destruction, hope and wisdom.

2. PLAYFUL FRAMING

The distinctive central sketch of this German book cover was drawn by the author, Milan Kundera. His playful style is reflected in the typography, which runs both horizontally and vertically to form a frame around the portrait.

3. METICULOUS MONTAGE

The precise photographic montage reflects this Spanish non-fiction book's scientific content and gives the reader a taste of what's inside. The images are grouped and spaced meticulously, resulting in a satisfying sense of visual order.

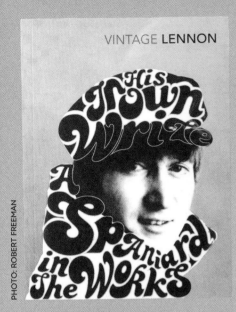

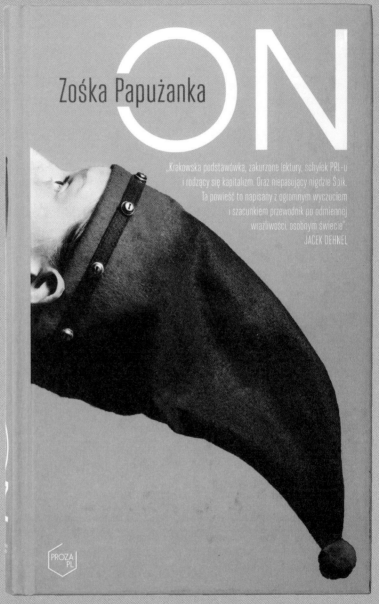

4. TYPOGRAPHIC OVERLAY

This design updates the cover photo of the 1964 edition by overlaying Lennon's hat and jacket with 60s-style lettering. This scrapbook feel chimes with the book's patchwork of stories, drawings, and poems.

5. A PICTURE OF WORDS

This cover for a 1928 book entitled *Kite* was created by Takehisa Yumeji, an influential avant-garde artist in Japan. The strong colour and graphic typography reflect Takehisa's interest in Modernist art trends of the time.

6. UNUSUAL ANGLES

The dramatic cover of this Polish novel uses a mix of ranged-right type and a strong diagonal to lead the eye over and down the entire cover. The author's name and book title intersect, creating a striking typographical effect.

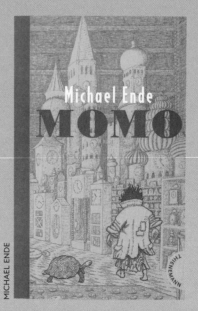

7. REPEATING MOTIFS

Designed for Penguin by Coralie Bickford-Smith, this clothbound cover features a trellis-like pattern created by repeating motifs of monkeys. The spaces created for text are so artfully executed that they seem like natural clearings in the forest.

8. CLASSIC COMBINATION

On the cover of this classic German children's book, the text is centred and placed in the top third, over the image. The central characters are also drawn in blue, forming a clear and pleasing visual connection between image and text.

9. PLAYING WITH PERSPECTIVE

By mimicking Andy Warhol's iconic soup can artwork, this Penguin cover communicates the theme of the book visually and in words. The text is manipulated to make the can look almost three-dimensional.

10. TEXT AND TEXTURE

The entire cover of this Swedish novel about settlers in 19th-century USA is designed to look like a tapestry, echoing the stitched samplers of the time. The text sits "underground", emphasizing the theme of

11. IMAGINED LANDSCAPE

Painted by the author, this cover image depicts Middle Earth, the book's imaginary setting. The hand-lettered text sits amidst the landscape and draws the eye into the image, inviting the reader to join the characters

12. THINKING SPACE

On this cover, Russian poet Osip Mandelstam is sketched in a meditative pose, overlaid with handwritten text. The large space between the title and image creates a pleasing sense of balance, while emphasizing

COMPOSITION }

To create successful layouts, you'll need to know about composition – putting all the elements together. Using a grid, the structure that underpins a layout, will give you confidence as you no longer face daunting blank space when you start to design. Learning how to balance the different weights of elements enables you to create harmony and order, and understanding the special considerations of designing for digital means you'll be able to compose layouts that work in any format.

CHOOSING AND USING A GRID

GRID BASICS

A grid consists of horizontal and vertical lines that divide the design area into sections. Almost all design is underpinned by some kind of grid. In some cases the grid supporting the layout is obvious, whereas in others it's used more sparingly, and only becomes clear on closer inspection.

This book was designed using both three- and four-column grids, depending on the content on each spread. This spread has three columns per page.

» Why use a grid?

A grid enables you to arrange elements in a logical way. By establishing rhythm and pace, the grid helps the audience to find the same type of information over a number of pages, and also means that you can work faster and more efficiently.

» Choosing a grid

The type of grid you choose will depend on factors such as the amount of content you have, the number of pages, and whether it is a print or online project. You can download grids that are ready to use, or set up your own (see overleaf).

» Breaking the rules

Sometimes, going "off grid" is the best strategy – to reinforce a particular meaning, or to break continuity and grab the reader's attention. As you become more confident, you will develop a sense of when it's appropriate to break the rules.

TYPES OF GRID

SINGLE COLUMN

The simplest grid consists of just one column. It is generally used for setting text-heavy documents, often with a continuous block of text that extends to multiple pages. Items such as page numbers or footnotes sit in the margin area, outside the grid.

SINGLE-COLUMN GRID

MULTIPLE COLUMNS

For print design, a page is normally divided into a number of columns. The more columns you have, the more options there are for organizing text and images in different ways. Altering the space between a grid's columns will also change the look and feel of a layout.

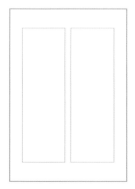

TWO-COLUMN GRID

MODULAR GRID

Modular grids have both columns and rows, so that the grid simultaneously operates vertically and horizontally. Each block is the same size and can be either square or rectangular. Spaces between blocks are also equal.

NINE-BLOCK MODULAR GRID

In design, a grid is a structure that sits invisibly underneath your layout and helps you to arrange elements in an organized way. When you design, use grids to help you maximize the meaning – and visual appeal – of layouts.

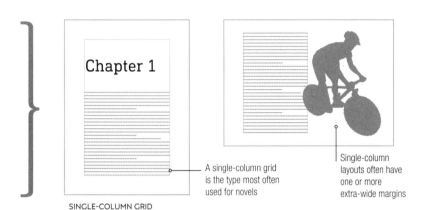

A single-column grid is the type most often used for novels

SINGLE-COLUMN GRID

Single-column layouts often have one or more extra-wide margins

If your design is landscape format, don't make the column too wide or text could be hard to read. Increase the text size if possible, and aim for a maximum of 60 characters per line.

THREE-COLUMN GRID

FOUR-COLUMN GRID

Cut-out images can break slightly out of the grid to create visual interest

Asymmetrical grids add visual interest, while keeping consistency and order across the layout.

NINE-BLOCK LAYOUT OPTIONS

A simple, nine-block grid offers many options for organizing a space in different ways. It is especially useful for layouts with lots of different elements and for highly visual content.

CREATE A PRINT GRID

SETTING UP A GRID

Creating a grid can be a useful stage in progressing your design. The process means that you have to think carefully about the outcome you are aiming for. Here's a checklist of things to think about or decide on when you create your working grid:

① DECIDE ON A FORMAT

Check the dimension of your chosen format and measure it carefully. Ideally, cut out a page and hold it in your hand to check you are happy with it. Then create your page and the grid within that.

② THINK ABOUT CONTENT

The content you are working with will influence your choice of grid. Make a list of the different elements you have in addition to normal body copy: this could include headings, different sizes of illustration, quotations, captions, or tables. A lot of elements might call for more flexibility, which usually means more modules or columns.

③ DO YOUR RESEARCH

Look through books and magazines for inspiration. With practice, you will be able to identify and replicate the grids underpinning layouts that you feel work well.

④ SET THE MARGINS

Set the margins around the page. If you are designing spreads – pages that face each other, as in the inside of a book or magazine – your margins need to allow for the gutter, which is the space between the pages when they are placed together. Usually, the right margin of the left-hand page will be wider than the left margin, and vice versa for the right-hand page.

⑤ SET COLUMNS OR BLOCKS

Decide on the number of columns or modules you want. Make sure you leave enough space between the columns, known as gutters, or your layouts will appear cramped.

⑥ SET THE BASELINE GRID

The horizontal lines running across the grid are known as the baseline grid. These guidelines help you to align different blocks of text.

ANATOMY OF A GRID

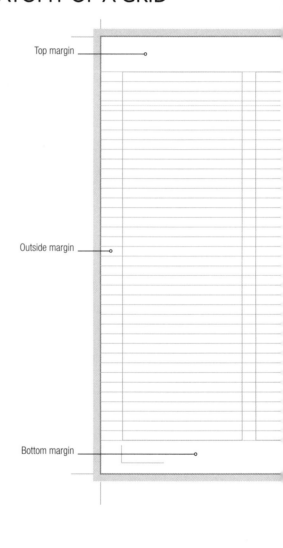

Top margin

Outside margin

Bottom margin

Most design software allows you to create your own grids. Getting to grips with grids will mean you can structure projects to your exact specifications, work more quickly, and create multiple layouts that look consistent and work together seamlessly.

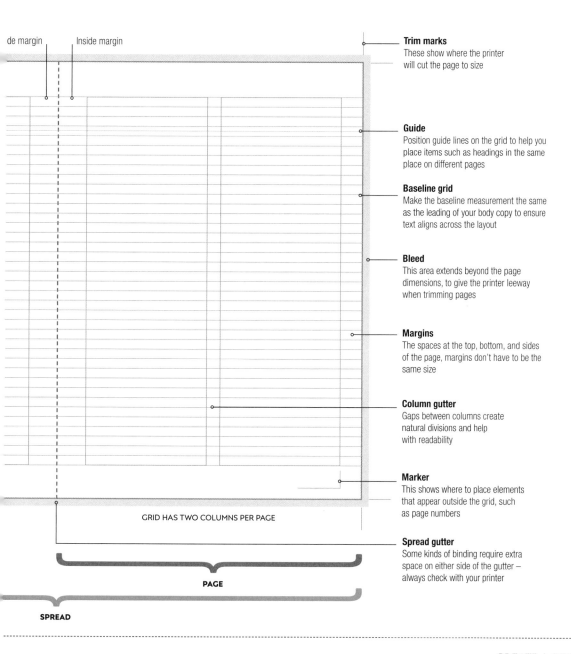

de margin

Inside margin

Trim marks
These show where the printer will cut the page to size

Guide
Position guide lines on the grid to help you place items such as headings in the same place on different pages

Baseline grid
Make the baseline measurement the same as the leading of your body copy to ensure text aligns across the layout

Bleed
This area extends beyond the page dimensions, to give the printer leeway when trimming pages

Margins
The spaces at the top, bottom, and sides of the page, margins don't have to be the same size

Column gutter
Gaps between columns create natural divisions and help with readability

Marker
This shows where to place elements that appear outside the grid, such as page numbers

Spread gutter
Some kinds of binding require extra space on either side of the gutter – always check with your printer

GRID HAS TWO COLUMNS PER PAGE

PAGE

SPREAD

USING ALIGNMENT

ALIGNMENT BASICS

Aligning is the lining up of two or more elements along a margin or other line. The line is usually not visible; it's implied by the arrangement of elements. Alignment is attractive – the eye is more drawn to the second graphic below, where shapes form a regular pattern.

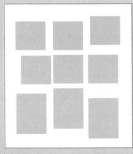

NON-ALIGNED ELEMENTS

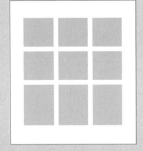

ALIGNED ELEMENTS

» Showing connections
Aligning a set of elements helps audiences understand that they are related to each other. For instance, if a picture needs a caption, aligning text with the edge of the image makes it clear that they are connected.

» Helping the flow
The reader shouldn't have to search for the next thing to look at. The order should be set by the designer, and be obvious and easy to follow. Alignment is a key way to indicate the flow of a design.

» Adding visual appeal
Aligned elements generally look more visually attractive on a layout – and the more engaged viewers are, the more likely they are to be receptive to your message.

» Using space efficiently
Alignment can help you fit more elements into a layout when space is tight – for instance, when designing for smartphones.

ALIGNING TEXT

Any text that's longer than a single line needs to be set out so that it aligns with itself at the start, finish, or through the centre of each line.

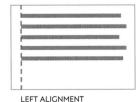

LEFT ALIGNMENT

LEFT-ALIGNED
Also known as ranged left or flush left, the text aligns along its left edge. This is the most common way to set text in Western languages, as the eye is used to reading from left to right.

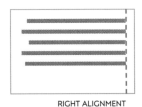

RIGHT ALIGNMENT

RIGHT-ALIGNED
Text that lines up on the right leads the eye across a page. It can be tiring to read in longer chunks, as the eye has to "search" for the start of each line.

CENTRED

CENTRE-ALIGNED
This describes alignment along a vertical axis through the middle of the text. It works best for shorter chunks of text at the top of a page, as it draws the eye down.

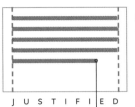

J U S T I F I E D

JUSTIFIED
Justified text aligns along both its left and right edges. Avoid justification for online use – as the text adjusts for different platforms, it can create large gaps between words that makes text hard to read.

Last line is left unjustified, so as not to leave ugly gaps between words

Humans are hardwired to respond to visual order. If we look at a collection of letters or shapes, we will always try to make visual sense of the jumble. Alignment is a useful design tool for delivering information in the ordered, organized way that viewers respond to best.

ALIGNING LAYOUTS

LEFT ALIGNMENT

The most popular way of aligning different elements in a layout is along a left-hand margin or line. This arrangement looks natural to an audience used to scanning from left to right, because this is how layouts are conventionally designed.

Line of alignment

LEFT-ALIGNED LAYOUT

The text blocks and heading on this landscape single page are all aligned to the left-hand margin, leaving space on the right for the three athletes to "run" into. This lends a dynamic feel to the layout.

CENTRE ALIGNMENT

Elements can be aligned along a line that runs through their centre. Centring can be tricky to use: text sometimes looks ragged and can also be hard to read, as each line starts in a different position. It works best if there is minimal text on a layout, or when one or more blocks of text are justified.

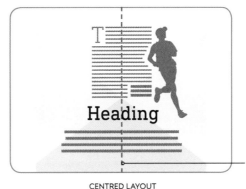

Line of alignment

CENTRED LAYOUT

Centring the elements creates space on both sides of this digital page. The symmetrical, almost static look may not be ideal for a layout that features a sporting activity.

RIGHT ALIGNMENT

This arrangement encourages the viewer to look across a whole layout, as the eye is drawn to the top right corner. It often works well with landscape formats. It's also useful to connect text to an image when they appear on the right-hand side of the layout.

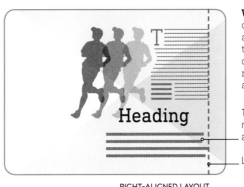

Text box aligns with right margin, while the text itself aligns with its own left edge

Line of alignment

RIGHT-ALIGNED LAYOUT

With the elements aligning on the right, the athletes are now heading against the left-to-right flow. This can create interest, but risks it looking as if they are running backwards.

SUMMER @THE FLOWER SHOP

NEWSLETTER

CONTACT/ORDERS

WIN OUR BOUQUET OF THE MONTH

We're celebrating the sunshine with this gorgeous bouquet. To be in with a **chance to win**, simply go to our prize draw page and enter your details...

I WANT TO WIN ▷

NEW IN STORE

These little beauties are just in, so why not buy a few and make a great group display? Don't forget to pick up our Cactus Care leaflet, **FREE** with every plant.

SHOP CACTI ▷

WEDDING PLANS?

Make an appointment now for a **FREE** consultation with our weddings team. Early-bird discounts on all orders for next year!

BOOK ME IN ▷

FUNKY FAKES

Our new range of artificial flowers has been a HUGE hit. This month, we're offering subscribers **10% discount** on all silk bouquets.

SHOP SILKS ▷

© The Flower Shop

Want to change how you receive emails?

UPDATE PREFERENCES OR UNSUBSCRIBE

VIEW THIS EMAIL IN BROWSER

CONTACT   RECOMMEND A FRIEND   ORDERS

FLOWER POWER

If, like this florist, you have products that are photogenic, it makes sense to let them shine. Here, the main photo both shows off the flowers and puts a human, happy face on the business. The newsletter's purpose is clear – to inform readers of new stock and special offers. Each story has its own call-to-action button, making it easy for the reader to find out more or buy items.

EMAIL WINDOW

SCROLL DOWN TO VIEW CONTENT

DESIGN AN **EMAIL NEWSLETTER**

A digital newsletter is an effective way to communicate with an audience. However, their popularity means that a newsletter must work hard to get noticed in a crammed inbox, and tempt the reader to engage with it.

THE BRIEF

This florist is launching a quarterly newsletter. The aim is to keep existing customers informed of special offers and news, and also to attract new customers by offering special discounts for subscribers.

JOB SPEC:

- Overall aim: design a newsletter template that can be used to create a regular news bulletin, as well as any one-off mailshots that the business owner may require.

- Convey relevant information: WHO is the newsletter from? WHAT information is it conveying? HOW can the customer enquire further, order, or make a purchase?

- The newsletter needs to be designed in keeping with the existing visual and verbal brand.

- The design needs to be engaging enough for people to notice it in their mailboxes, and be tempted to read further.

- The design should be viewable on different platforms, such as mobile phone, tablet, or desktop.

THE TOOLKIT

A newsletter must have strong visual appeal – audiences engage far more with visual material than with text. If you haven't already, get into the habit of taking pictures of your daily work – they will also be useful to keep your profile high on social media. Keep colour palettes and graphic devices firmly on-brand; however, fonts should be standard web fonts to ensure they can be read on different platforms.

PHOTOS

PHOTOS TO ILLUSTRATE NEWS STORIES

SOCIAL MEDIA ICONS

Clickable icons allow viewers to find you easily on social media

COLOUR PALETTE

SAGE
R181 G187 B157

PINK
R192 G172 B181

BLACK
R43 G38 B32

LOGO

THE FLOWER SHOP

TYPEFACES

Harmonia Sans Pro Light

Harmonia Sans Pro Regular

Harmonia Sans Pro Semibold

THE DESIGN PROCESS

CHOOSE A TEMPLATE

The easiest way to create and send a newsletter is via an e-marketing company. These one-stop services offer a range of design templates, as well as managing your contacts database, sending out newsletters, and tracking and analysing responses. For this project, the designer chose a two-column format with a full-width header area at the top.

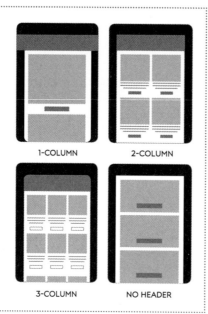

1-COLUMN   2-COLUMN

3-COLUMN   NO HEADER

OFFER A CLEAR CALL TO ACTION

The purpose of any newsletter is to get readers to engage with the content. Call-to-action buttons clearly inform the viewer how they can buy an item or see more information.

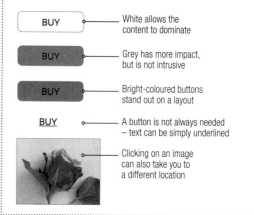

BUY — White allows the content to dominate

BUY — Grey has more impact, but is not intrusive

BUY — Bright-coloured buttons stand out on a layout

BUY — A button is not always needed – text can be simply underlined

Clicking on an image can also take you to a different location

PLAN THE CONTENT

The newsletter has three distinct areas that you need to plan and design:

The header acts like the masthead of a newspaper and should look the same on every newsletter you send out. It should contain the logo, and be an inviting, instantly recognizable entry point for the reader.

Content This will depend on your aims and whether you have a single items of news, or several. Here are some guidelines for making the most of content:

1. Make the heading to each story succinct and inviting, to tempt viewers to read on.

2. Around two sentences per story is enough – people are turned off by long, dense text.

3. Images are essential. Ensure they are sharp, high-quality, and on-brand.

The footer rounds things off and reinforces your brand. Include the logo and contact details, links to social media feeds, plus copyright and unsubscribing information.

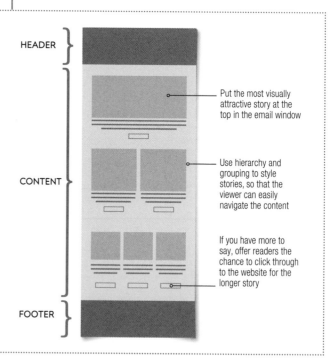

HEADER

CONTENT

FOOTER

Put the most visually attractive story at the top in the email window

Use hierarchy and grouping to style stories, so that the viewer can easily navigate the content

If you have more to say, offer readers the chance to click through to the website for the longer story

ALTERNATIVE DESIGNS

These two examples show that you can achieve different but equally striking designs while staying on-brand. Experiment with templates to find one that works best with your content.

"Order" buttons at the top and bottom of the page makes the buying process easy

A FINE BALANCE

This design allows for an introduction – a place for the business owner to address the reader directly with friendly, personal text. White margins round the content and between stories add visual breathing space and give the layout a relaxed, breezy feel, in keeping with the subject matter.

Call-out buttons are all the same colour, so viewers can find them easily

SHORT AND SWEET

This design uses full-width coloured panels to enclose the stories. Minimal text lets the images dominate – long, wordy newsletters inevitably go straight into the mail bin. Here, there are only two stories, keeping the message simple and clear for the reader.

GROUPING WITHIN LAYOUTS

THE PSYCHOLOGY OF GROUPING

The human brain strives to find order in the bombardment of data it receives. Researchers in human perception have established certain principles of how we tend to group and organize information, which are useful for graphic designers to bear in mind.

SIMPLIFYING INFORMATION

When we see this graphic, we simplify the data so that we see the arrangement of lines as a recognizable shape.

We see a square, not an arrangement of four lines

LOOKING FOR CONTINUITY

We look for continuity when viewing images – the eye will follow smooth, continuous lines and patterns rather than jagged or disjointed ones.

We see a smooth arch and a straight line, not a series of shorter,more jagged paths

SEEKING CLOSURE

The brain supplies "missing" information when faced with what it perceives as an incomplete shape or image.

Most people see an arrangement of triangles and circles, even though the shapes are not fully drawn

WAYS OF GROUPING

There are various ways to show that elements are part of a group within a layout. Your choice of method will depend on factors such as the amount of space you have and the complexity of the layout.

ENCLOSING ELEMENTS

One of the simplest and most immediate ways to show that things belong together is to fence them in. You could do this by drawing a simple border round the elements, or by sitting them within a coloured panel.

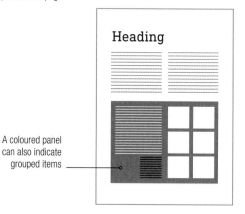

The border shows which elements form their own group within the page

A coloured panel can also indicate grouped items

Arranging elements in groups is a tool, often used along with alignment, that designers use to make sense of layouts. By making clear visual links between related items, you guide your audience so they can follow your message and meaning.

USING SPACE

Proximity is a widely used principle of grouping. It simply means that the closer elements are to each other, the more likely the viewer is to see them as a part of a group.

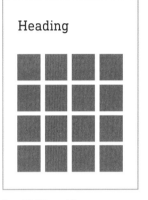

Two groups – We perceive this layout as containing two groups – the wide central space marks a clear separation between sets of elements.

Four groups – Here, the brain has to work a little harder to find connections. However, most viewers will perceive four groups on the layout.

Equal billing – The spaces between all the elements are the same. We assume that they comprise a single group, each square having equal importance.

USING SIMILARITY

Another way in which the brain groups visual information is by similarity. Items that share the same characteristics will be usually seen as having a connection.

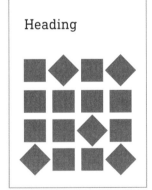

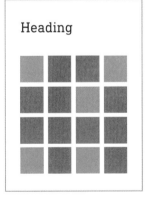

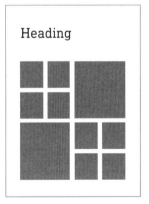

Grouping by shape – In this grid of squares, the rotated shapes stand out clearly as a sub-group.

Grouping by colour – Colour is a potent way of showing a link. If there are different types of similarity on a page, colour is often the one that will dominate the others.

Grouping by size – Items of a similar size within a group will often be assumed to have a connection. The larger and smaller squares form two separate groups.

ACHIEVE HARMONY AND BALANCE

UNDERSTANDING VISUAL WEIGHT

Obviously, the things that we look at on page or screen have no actual weight, but in art and design, the term "visual weight" describes the force or attraction that an element exerts on the viewer. The greater something's visual weight, the more the eye is attracted to it. Various attributes affect an element's visual weight, such as size, tone, shape, and texture.

Larger items have more weight than smaller ones.

Darker tones appear "heavier" than lighter ones.

A regular shape conveys more visual weight than an irregular form.

An element with texture will seem weightier than an untextured one.

WAYS TO ACHIEVE BALANCE

Here are some of the factors you should consider when thinking about ways to handle different weights of elements in a layout.

SYMMETRICAL BALANCE

Using symmetry – arranging elements in the same way on either side of a central line – is a sure way to give both sides of the design equal weight. Symmetry looks stable and controlled, but too much can be monotonous.

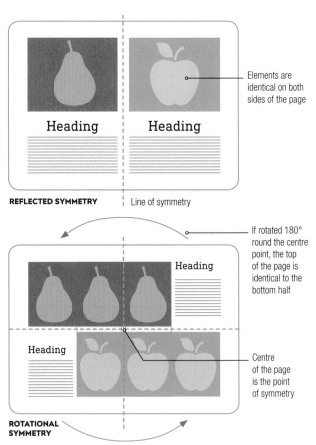

Elements are identical on both sides of the page

REFLECTED SYMMETRY   Line of symmetry

If rotated 180° round the centre point, the top of the page is identical to the bottom half

Centre of the page is the point of symmetry

ROTATIONAL SYMMETRY

Just as a set of scales needs equal weights to balance, a successful layout needs to have an equal spread of its components. Visual balance describes how well the various elements are distributed so that they balance each other out across the layout.

ASYMMETRICAL BALANCE

Asymmetry attracts the eye, and an asymmetrical design can be dynamic and attention-grabbing. You need to pay a little more attention to ensuring you achieve balance than with a symmetrical layout, but the result will be more lively and engaging.

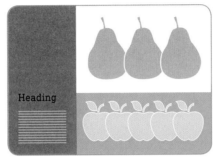

A grid based on the golden ratio will help you to balance an asymmetrical layout.

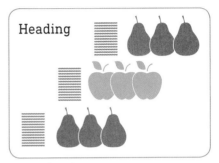

Staggered sections encourage the eye to move across the space.

BALANCING SIZES

Large images add interest and drama to a layout. It's important to balance them, or the page can look lopsided. Add compensating weight to other elements, for example by using colour or texture.

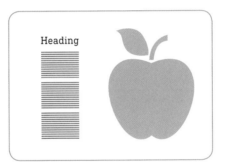

One large image can balance several smaller elements.

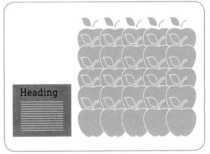

Lots of small items will carry the same weight and impact as a single large one.

BALANCING COLOURS

As well as darker tones carrying more weight than lighter ones, warmer colours will appear weightier than cooler ones. For example, a warm colour can be an effective accent within a large area of cool colour.

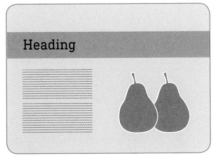

A full-page expanse of cool blue provides a good visual balance for the smaller, warm orange elements.

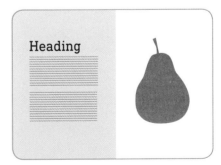

Weightier colours such as warm orange seem to "advance" towards the eye. Cool blue recedes, so is a good choice as a background.

DESIGN FOR PHONES AND SOCIAL MEDIA

DESIGNING FOR DIGITAL

Increasingly the trend in graphic design is for the "digital first" (or "mobile first") approach. This means designing with digital screens, and hand-held screens in particular, in mind, before considering print. There are real advantages to this approach:

» Digital dominates
The most common way now for people to access and search for information is via phones and tablets: to reach your audience effectively, you can't afford to ignore digital media and social channels.

» Reaching the right target
Social media is brilliant for reaching a target audience: for instance, if you are selling hand-knitted baby clothes, you can look for individuals and groups who are far more likely than average to be interested in your products.

» Quick and cheap
Digital designs can be changed almost instantly, and as often as you like. Updating or refreshing a page, and correcting mistakes is easier and cheaper than if you are using print media.

» Easier to adapt for print
It's easier to reconfigure digital designs to make them suitable for printing than the other way round. Scaling up your work will present fewer challenges than trying to fit an existing design into the small space and narrow format allowed on a phone.

DIGITAL COMPOSITION
USING IMAGES

As with all design, any pictures you use must visually represent your brand. Applying digital first principles, ensure the image works at a small size by keeping content simple, with uncluttered backgrounds and a clear focus on the subject.

Keep key parts of the image in the centre, as images can be cropped on social media sites

Crop in tightly to show detail and lead the eye to the heart of the image

LANDSCAPE AND PORTRAIT

Your design template will automatically rearrange the layout when the device is turned onto its side. This is known as responsive layout, and is explained on page 175. Always make sure that your design works in either format.

Type within images is not responsive, so will not resize. Check it is readable on small screens

Many people will see your brand or project for the first time on a phone, so it's crucial that your designs work in this format, and on corresponding social media. In addition to the general design principles covered in this chapter, here are some additional considerations for designing for mobiles.

SOCIAL MEDIA

By far the most common way to view social media is on a hand-held screen, so always keep the small format in mind when choosing and designing content.

» Keep it simple

Go for strong graphics and minimal text. Research shows that people respond far more to content with images than without, so keep content highly visual, to grab the attention of casual browsers and tempt them to click through to get the longer story.

» Make it yours

Customize your space as much as you're allowed: include your logo and ensure backgrounds, colours, and, where possible, fonts, reflect your brand. Make your look consistent across different social media platforms.

» Read the specs

Every social media platform has different specifications for size and orientation of content – and these frequently change. Always design material to the exact dimensions stated, or it may not display as you'd like.

» Get help for apps

For most small projects, using social media is cheaper and often more efficient than designing a dedicated app. If you are considering developing an app, get advice from a specialist designer.

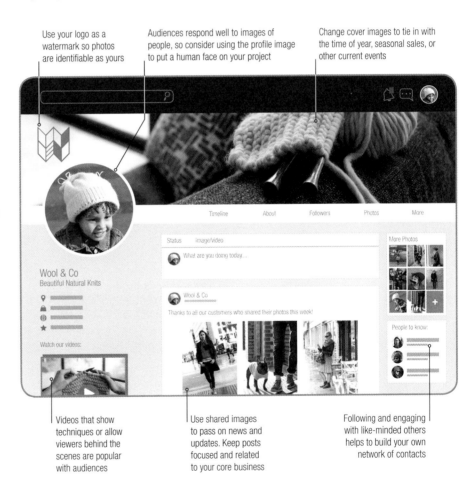

Use your logo as a watermark so photos are identifiable as yours

Audiences respond well to images of people, so consider using the profile image to put a human face on your project

Change cover images to tie in with the time of year, seasonal sales, or other current events

Videos that show techniques or allow viewers behind the scenes are popular with audiences

Use shared images to pass on news and updates. Keep posts focused and related to your core business

Following and engaging with like-minded others helps to build your own network of contacts

WEBSITE COMPOSITION

WEBSITE BASICS

Most people don't build their websites from scratch, they use templates and themes provided by a website platform. These companies provide ready-made layouts that you can drop your content into. They do all the coding for you, and many also offer additional services such as hosting and shopping facilities. This leaves you free to concentrate on the look and content, making sure it's right for your project and brand.

TEMPLATE CHECKLIST

Thinking about what you want your website to do will help you choose a format and layout from the templates available.

» **Consider the type of content**
Will your content consist mainly of images, or longer sections of text? Refer to "Types of website" on this page to help you determine the type of website you'll be operating.

» **Plan the content**
Calculate how many pages you'll need and roughly map out content, noting any different features you'll require. You might find it useful to sketch out a wireframe (see page 176). Look for templates that offer the elements you've identified.

» **Choose a template to match your style**
It's crucial that your website will match your brand's visual style. Make sure that you can change a template's typefaces and colours to reflect your brand identity.

TYPES OF WEBSITE

SINGLE-PAGE SITE

A simple, one-page site that acts as a digital business card, might be all you need. Displaying contact details and information about the service or company, and a contact form for enquiries, this type of site requires little maintenance or updating.

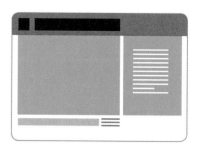

PORTFOLIO

A website can be an effective digital portfolio or CV, where you display your work for others to browse. Usually, a viewer scrolls through the content, and clicks on an image to bring up an enlarged version.

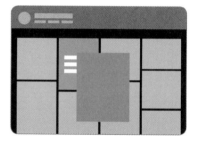

E-COMMERCE

An online shop needs to showcase your products, and offer an easy interface and trustworthy payment process. You can choose your website theme to fit your specification, and add payment facilities too.

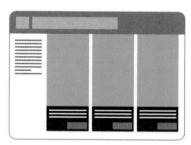

BLOG

A blog is an online journal, with the most recent posts displayed first and a searchable list of past posts. A blog is typically quite text-heavy. Blogs can be stand-alone websites or sections within an existing site.

A successful website follows the same principles of all good graphic design, but there are specific issues to consider. Your digital shop window needs to be easy to navigate, viewable at different sizes and formats, and a pleasure to use.

RESPONSIVE LAYOUT

The template you choose will be responsive – which means that the layout automatically rearranges to fit the format and platform it's being viewed in. So on a desktop, a page will be seen at full scale and across the width of the screen; on a tablet or smart phone, the software will automatically stack the materials into blocks or modules.

Responsive layouts work by calculating sizes for the new format as a percentage of the original layout: items are therefore resized in proportion, so that as far as possible, they retain the same relationships to each other.

It is crucial that a composition works in the smallest format, which is why many designers now design "mobile first" – see page 172 for more on this.

DESKTOP

A 12-column grid is a good choice for web design as it gives so much flexibility. It can operate as a 6-, 4-, 3- or 2-column grid, altering as the screen width changes on different devices.

| 1x12 |
| 2x6 |
| 3x4 |
| 4x3 |

Grid can be divided in different ways

TABLET

When the same site is viewed on a tablet, the grid reduces in size and operates as a 6-column structure. The content then re-arranges itself within the grid, keeping the original proportions where possible.

PHONE

On a mobile screen, the grid reduces even further so it effectively has two or just one column. The menu bar, if there was one, disappears and is replaced with the "hamburger" device, which displays a drop-down menu when clicked.

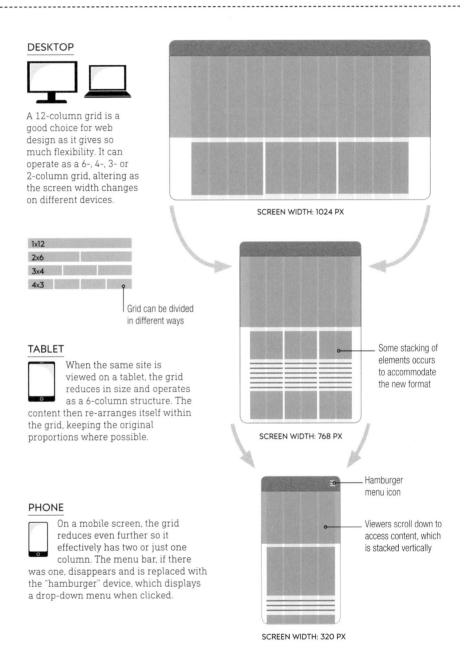

SCREEN WIDTH: 1024 PX

SCREEN WIDTH: 768 PX

Some stacking of elements occurs to accommodate the new format

Hamburger menu icon

Viewers scroll down to access content, which is stacked vertically

SCREEN WIDTH: 320 PX

WIREFRAMES FOR WEBSITES

HOW TO MAKE A WIREFRAME

A good wireframe will help you solve problems at an earlier stage of the project, saving time and money, and leading to a better finished website. Here's how to do it:

① CLARIFY YOUR AIMS

As with all projects, ensure before you start that you are clear about the purpose of your website and who will be using it. Plan with the user in mind, rather than reflecting the way that you see your project. Look at competitors' websites and others that you like, taking note of things that you feel work well.

② DECIDE ON A MEDIUM

Your purpose in wireframing is not to make design decisions, but to plan content and decide where to locate it within the website. Start by deciding on the medium for the wireframe: you could sketch with pencil and paper, use the computer to make your own rough layout, or use a free wireframe template that you can find easily online.

③ PLAN THE HOMEPAGE

The crucial element on the homepage is the menu: easy navigation should be at the heart of all decisions. Try to keep menu items to a minimum; can you combine different pages within the same section? Do you need sub-pages that require an additional click to reach? Other homepage elements could be social media links or a search facility.

④ MAP OUT THE CONTENT

Plan out the rest of the pages, showing how they link to the homepage and to other pages if appropriate. It might be useful to keep in mind the "three-click rule", the web-designers' adage that the audience should never have to click more than three times to reach their destination. While this is not always possible, your aim is always to make the user's experience as easy and pleasurable as possible.

ANATOMY OF A WIREFRAME

This example shows a wireframe for a charity website. The aims are to inform supporters and service users of activities, to attract donations, and to recruit volunteers and supporters. The wireframe helps to work out how to separate these functions, so users can easily find what they need.

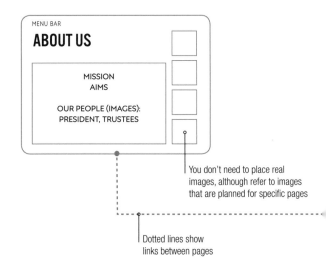

You don't need to place real images, although refer to images that are planned for specific pages

Dotted lines show links between pages

A wireframe is a simple plan of your website. Its main purpose is to help you work out how it will function by showing how the content will be organized, and by mapping the connections between the website's different sections and pages.

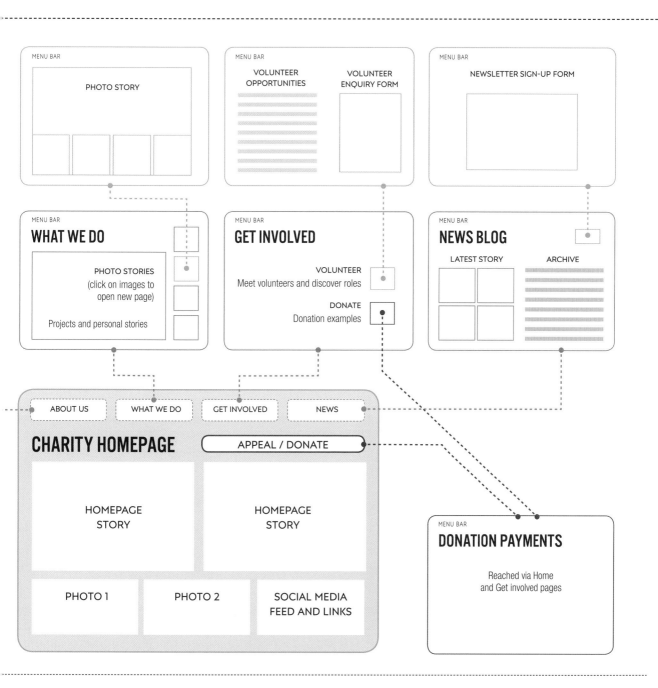

Clicking on the menu bar takes the viewer down to the relevant section of the page

STRONG AND SIMPLE

This design suits the subject perfectly – it's lean, muscular and ultra-efficient. With minimal text, colour, and decoration, the focus is very much on the images, which give an inviting taste of what customers can look forward to if they sign up.

The red of the fixed menu bar adds an accent of warm colour, and also provides balance for the larger areas of grey, which carry less visual weight

Another red banner forms the footer, anchoring the design and providing links to social media feeds

DESIGN A **WEB HOMEPAGE**

Almost any business or project benefits from having its own website. An official online presence reassures customers and allows access to the most up-to-date information about your products, services, or activities.

THE BRIEF

For this project, a self-employed fitness coach is ready to expand the business by establishing a company, partnering with other professionals, and launching an online marketing campaign. The website will be at the heart of the new company's activities.

JOB SPEC:

- Overall aim: to create a simple but effective website to showcase the services offered and attract new customers.
- Convey all the basic information in an accessible, easy-to-use format: WHAT kind of business is it? WHO are the people behind it? WHAT services are offered? HOW can prices, schedules and similar information be accessed? HOW can a customer sign up?
- To reinforce the brand identity by its use of colour, type, images, and language.
- Appeal to the identified target market – young, aspirational, busy, and health-conscious professionals.

THE TOOLKIT

The watchword of this design toolkit is simplicity. The bold, graphic logo device, the minmal colour palette with just one accent colour, and the limited use of fonts all contribute to the pared-down, calm authority of the brand. The photos are key – carefully shot and styled to chime with the brand, they convey information, while giving the audience positive outcomes they can aspire to.

PHOTOS

COLOUR PALETTE

RED	WHITE	BLACK
R201 G64 B74	R255 G255 B255	R0 G0 B0

SOCIAL MEDIA LINKS

TYPEFACES

Open Sans Regular
Open Sans Bold
Lato light
Lato Bold

LOGO

 BODY**WISE**

THE DESIGN PROCESS

DO THE RESEARCH

The company has identified its target customers – now the task is to find out which design approaches appeal most to them.

Look at competitors in your field – what are they doing well that you could learn from? Look beyond your local area – it could be that there are trends in other countries that haven't reached yours yet.

Analyse companies outside your sector that engage successfully with your market – from dating sites to drinks companies. As well as design factors, note the language and tone of voice they use.

Ask the audience – this company polled existing customers to find out their favourite (and least-liked) sites and products. It also conducted first-hand research to gauge the reaction to its initial ideas and designs.

« **RESEARCH YOUR AUDIENCE** – SEE PAGE 24

THINK ABOUT FONTS

If you are using a website-building platform, the typefaces will all be web-safe. This means that viewers will see your page just as you designed it, even if they don't have that font loaded onto their device. The most popular free web typefaces are:

 Open sans This typeface has excellent legibility in different sizes and formats and was the choice for this website.

 Roboto Described as modern and friendly, Roboto's rounded forms and versatility make it a popular choice.

 Lato With a strong structure that conveys stability, Lato is the typeface used for the company's wordmark.

« **CHOOSE A FONT** – SEE PAGE 60

① ② ③

PLAN THE LAYOUT

A long, scrollable homepage is a popular choice in website design, because it's easy for viewers to find information without having to open multiple pages. The top of the page (Section A) is the website's "shop window", so it needs to grab attention. When designing a website like this, make sure that as the viewer scrolls down, the menu bar stays in place at the top of the page, for easy navigation.

SECTION A

SECTION B

SECTION C

SECTION B

SECTION C.

Section A represents what the viewer sees when they log on. Use compelling images and keep text to a minimum for instant impact

Menu bar stays in place as the viewer scrolls down

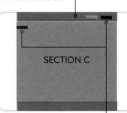

SECTION C

Viewers can choose either to scroll down or use the menu bar to jump directly to a section of the page

» ALTERNATIVE DESIGN

This website is built on a masonry (or Pinterest-style) grid, which consists of columns with rows of unequal heights. This creates an attractive, asymmetric pattern of images, which encourages the viewer to look – and scroll – down. This is an effective layout if you have a lot of good-quality pictures to show off. Achieving this super-streamlined look means there is almost no room for text. You'll need more pages if you opt for this showcase approach.

Hamburger menu accesses the drop-down menu

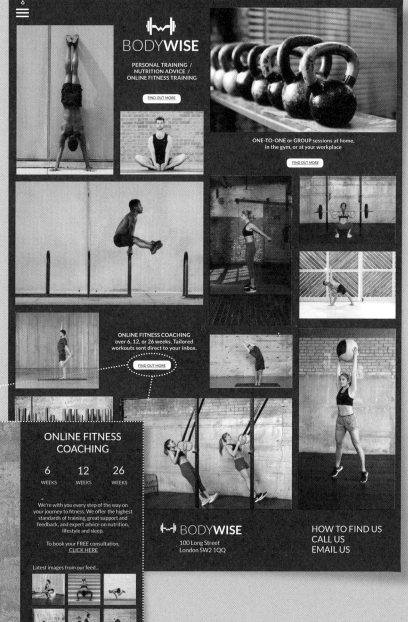

BODY**WISE**

PERSONAL TRAINING /
NUTRITION ADVICE /
ONLINE FITNESS TRAINING

FIND OUT MORE

ONE-TO-ONE or GROUP sessions at home,
in the gym, or at your workplace

FIND OUT MORE

ONLINE FITNESS COACHING
over 6, 12, or 26 weeks. Tailored
workouts sent direct to your inbox.

FIND OUT MORE

ONLINE FITNESS COACHING

6	12	26
WEEKS	WEEKS	WEEKS

We're with you every step of the way on
your journey to fitness. We offer the highest
standards of training, great support and
feedback, and expert advice on nutrition,
lifestyle and sleep.

To book your FREE consultation,
CLICK HERE

Latest images from our feed...

BODY**WISE**

BODY**WISE**
100 Long Street
London SW2 1QQ

HOW TO FIND US
CALL US
EMAIL US

« NEW PAGES

Viewers click on call-to-action buttons to open new pages and access more information.

COMPOSITION IN WEBSITES

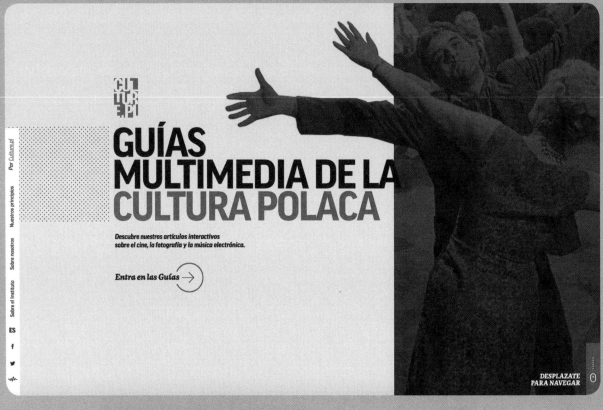

1. DRAMATIC ASYMMETRY

An asymmetrical layout, based on the golden ratio, creates drama for this multilingual guide to Polish culture. The dynamism is boosted by elements breaking out of their boundaries: the dancers' arms and text spill beyond their areas.

2. EASY NAVIGATION

In this user-friendly Japanese layout, the fixed vertical navigation bar can be made constantly visible and accessible as the user scrolls through the content. The main image is not a still, but a video that plays on a loop, like a GIF.

3. MONOCHROME MINIMALISM

In this pared-back layout for an art installation, the mesmeric video-screen background is the perfect foil for the bold, white call to action, as well as reflecting the theme of the installation itself.

4. SHOPFRONT

The entrepreneur behind Know & Love designed their website so that it invites the viewer in and is easy to browse. The use of simple cropping brings small details to the fore, emphasizing the brand's focus on hand-crafted products.

5. SPLIT SCREEN

A split-screen layout is ideal for giving equal weight to different elements – in this example of a German site, Bose's two product lines: speakers and headphones. Tightly cropped, monochrome photos create drama and impact.

6. VISUAL GRID

A clickable grid layout is a powerful way to showcase content of equal hierarchy in an easily accessible format. This global design resource offers endless possibilities with an infinitely variable combination of columns, sizes, and spacing.

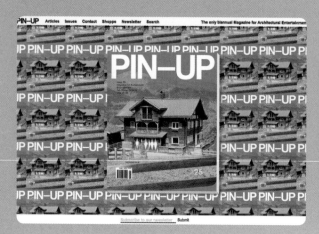

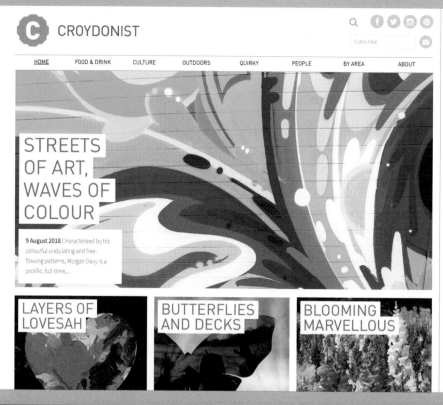

7. MAXIMALIST

A maximalist approach can result in an attention-grabbing and unforgettable design. Here, multiple images of the latest issue of the magazine fill the screen; the viewer then scrolls down to access the content

8. DIAGONAL DYNAMISM

Diagonal section breaks boost the visual interest and inject energy into this layout. This dynamic composition perfectly reflects the snapshots of the high-octane activities offered by the adventure company

9. COLOURFUL CONTENT

Striking images combined with quirky title copy are given centre stage on this blog about local culture, inviting the reader to click through. The navigation bar sits discreetly under the title to ensure the content gets all the attention

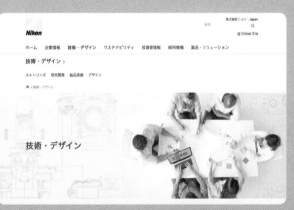

10. SINGLE IMAGE

This layout is based around a strong full-screen image of the product it is promoting. The photo's pink/black colours are picked up in the heading and call-to-action buttons, making a clear, consistent brand statement.

11. PARALLAX SCROLLING

In this example, showcasing the evolution of the Porsche car, a parallax scrolling technique creates an immersive, interactive experience as a new image gradually moves over the previous one as the user scrolls down.

12. ILLUSION OF DEPTH

The combination of overhead photography and flat illustration used in this camera brand's Japanese website creates an effective illusion of depth. It also highlights both the technical and creative aspects of photography.

PRODUCING YOUR DESIGNS }

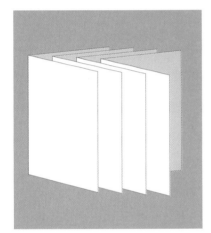

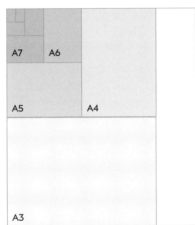

A7 A6

A5 A4

A3

ADVICE AND RESOURCES]

You need some practical knowledge to complement your newly acquired design skills. Knowing when and how to work with creative, print, and tech professionals is essential, and you should also make sure you prepare work thoroughly for either printing or online publishing. With advice on how to access free resources, and information on everything from paper sizes to copyright and colour swatches, you have the tools to see your work successfully through to completion.

SETTING UP: CHOOSING A COMPUTER

WHICH COMPUTER IS BEST?

Although most professional designers use a Mac, a PC with the right specification is fine too. Before you make a decision, consider the following advantages and disadvantages.

APPLE MAC

- Design-industry standard
- High-quality graphics
- Simple user interface
- Compatible with other Apple devices
- Fewer viruses
- Takes up less space
- More expensive
- Cannot be upgraded as easily as a PC

OR

PC

- Generally cheaper
- Large range of product options
- Easier to upgrade
- Broader choice of apps
- Colleagues are likely to have PCs
- Touch-screen monitor options
- Laptops can convert to tablets

DESKTOP OR LAPTOP?

Although desktop computers and laptops are comparable in performance, how and where you work will determine which is best for you.

Space If your home or office workspace is small, a laptop might be preferable, as it will take up less space.

Portability Is it important for you to be able to work in different locations? If so, a laptop may be best.

Screen size Desktops often have bigger screens, making it much easier to work on large or complex layouts.

Power source A laptop has a battery so can be operated away from a power source for short lengths of time.

SPECIFICATION CHECKLIST

Whatever computer you choose, you need to make sure it has a high enough specification for the job. Here are a few things to look out for.

MEMORY (RAM)

The higher a machine's RAM (random access memory), the more efficient it is at operating with multiple programs open. Aim for at least 8GB.

PERIPHERALS CHECKLIST

Devices that connect to a computer are known as "peripherals". Some, such as a printer, are likely to be essential. Others can help you work more efficiently, creatively, or safely.

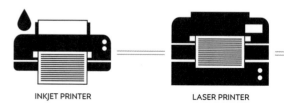

INKJET PRINTER   LASER PRINTER

PRINTER

When choosing a printer, you'll need to think about what you print, how often, and how much you're willing to spend.

- **Inkjet printers** are most common: they tend to be cheaper than laser printers, and are better for printing images. However, price per print can be high as ink cartridges are expensive and need to be replaced frequently.

- **Laser printers** are best for printing high-quality text. They are more expensive to buy, but can handle high volumes and are much quicker. The cost per print is lower than with inkjets, as they use less ink and generally require less maintenance.

All graphic designers work on a computer. You don't need to spend a fortune on the latest technology, but to produce high-quality designs you will need the right tools for the job. Spend wisely on hardware, and ensure it has the specifications you need.

PROCESSOR (CPU) SPEED

CPU speed determines how fast your computer works. Ideally, it should be 1GHz or above, and it should also be a multi-core processor, either dual or quad.

MONITOR SIZE

Monitor size is measured diagonally from corner to corner. If space isn't an issue, choose as large a screen as you can – at least 55cm (21.5in).

SCREEN RESOLUTION

The number of pixels that make up a screen is known as resolution. Higher resolution gives sharper definition. Choose at least 1280 x 800.

STORAGE CAPACITY

Your data is stored in your computer's hard drive and its capacity is measured in "bytes". You'll need a minimum of 1TB, but you can easily add more.

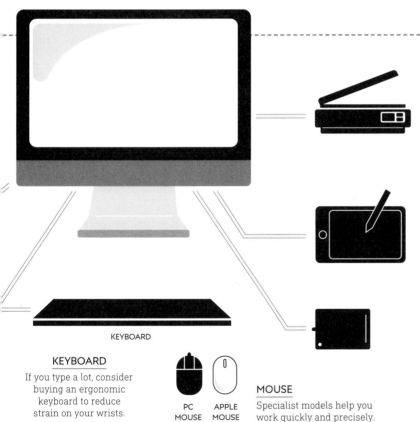

SCANNER

Many printers or smartphone apps scan text documents well (*see* page 211), but higher-quality results may require a separate scanner. Choose one with high resolution (at least 4800ppi for artworks), and ensure it is large enough for your needs.

GRAPHICS TABLET AND STYLUS

You can use a stylus to "draw" onto a touch-sensitive pad connected to your computer, like using pen and paper. Some people find a stylus is easier to use than a mouse and puts less strain on wrists and hands.

EXTERNAL HARD DRIVE

It's almost inevitable that, at some point, hardware will fail, files will corrupt, or you will lose your laptop. You can set your machine to automatically save copies of your work to an external hard drive. Another option is to back up continuously to the "cloud" – a remote server accessed online.

KEYBOARD

KEYBOARD

If you type a lot, consider buying an ergonomic keyboard to reduce strain on your wrists.

PC MOUSE   APPLE MOUSE

MOUSE

Specialist models help you work quickly and precisely.

SETTING UP: SOFTWARE AND YOUR WORKSPACE

CHOOSING YOUR SOFTWARE

There are many options when it comes to graphic design software – from professional programs, to cheap and even free substitutes (*see* pages 210–211). Choose your software depending on your needs. You might want to practise with free versions and upgrade if needed, for example. No matter which tool you choose, you'll need to invest time in learning to use it.

DESIGN SOFTWARE CHECKLIST

PAGE LAYOUT

Used for: combining text and graphics to design layouts. Many word-processing systems have page-layout options built in, but dedicated software, such as Adobe InDesign, gives you a much higher level of control over precise details like kerning and tracking (*see* page 55).

Examples include:
- Adobe InDesign
- Scribus
- Lucidpress

IMAGE EDITING

Used for: digitally altering or enhancing images. Though different programs have different tools and capabilities, even the most basic image-editing software should enable you to crop, adjust colour and brightness, and add or delete parts of the image (*see* page 99).

Examples include:
- Adobe Photoshop
- PaintShop Pro
- Affinity Photo

VECTOR EDITOR

Used for: editing and creating scalable graphics (*see* page 116), painting with brushes, and illustration. Though you are able to create simple vectors using some page-layout programs, vector-specific software tends to be more powerful. Some can also be used for animation.

Examples include:
- Adobe Illustrator
- CorelDRAW
- Affinity Designer

WEB DESIGN

Used for: creating and designing websites and web pages for both desktop and mobile. Some web-design programs require you to have at least a basic knowledge of code; however, many enable you to focus purely on the front-end design. Some are also web-hosting platforms.

Examples include:
- Adobe Dreamweaver
- Adobe Spark
- Sketch

FONT MANAGEMENT

Used for: browsing, downloading, and organizing fonts. If you need easy access to a large number of fonts, specialist software keeps your computer working efficiently by only activating fonts when you need them. You can also use such software to explore and buy different fonts.

Examples include:
- Adobe Fonts
- Google Fonts
- FontBase

Graphic design software tends to be very sophisticated, with a price tag to match, but there are many alternatives on a broad scale of cost and complexity. You also need to consider your work environment. With a bit of planning, even the smallest space can be functional, inspiring, and ergonomic.

SETTING UP YOUR WORKSPACE

Ideally, you should have a space dedicated to your work, whether you have a spare room to convert into a design studio or just a corner for a desk. The guidelines shown here will help you create a workspace that encourages creativity, efficiency, and safety.

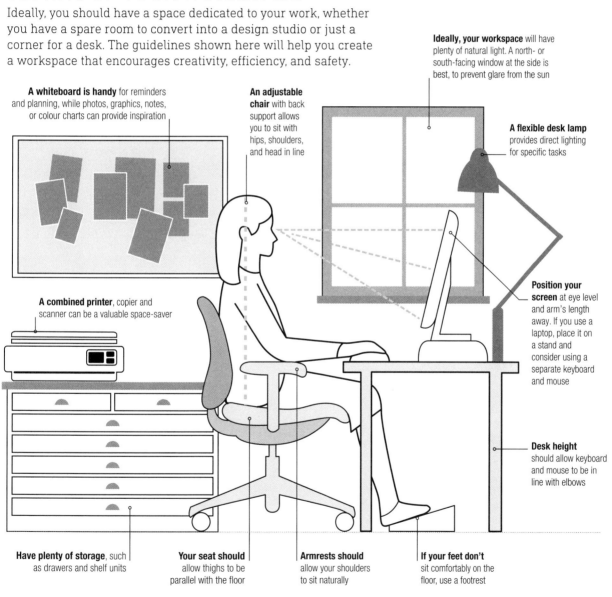

Ideally, your workspace will have plenty of natural light. A north- or south-facing window at the side is best, to prevent glare from the sun

A whiteboard is handy for reminders and planning, while photos, graphics, notes, or colour charts can provide inspiration

An adjustable chair with back support allows you to sit with hips, shoulders, and head in line

A flexible desk lamp provides direct lighting for specific tasks

A combined printer, copier and scanner can be a valuable space-saver

Position your screen at eye level and arm's length away. If you use a laptop, place it on a stand and consider using a separate keyboard and mouse

Desk height should allow keyboard and mouse to be in line with elbows

Have plenty of storage, such as drawers and shelf units

Your seat should allow thighs to be parallel with the floor

Armrests should allow your shoulders to sit naturally

If your feet don't sit comfortably on the floor, use a footrest

PLANNING A LARGER PRINT PROJECT

SIMPLE STEPS TO PLANNING SUCCESS

Unlike single-page or double-sided projects such as business cards or leaflets, multi-page projects require careful thought and planning in terms of structure and content, as well as project management.

STEP 1
COUNT YOUR PAGES

Your first step will be to work out the total number of pages you need. Designs with multiple pages are printed as sheets of four or eight pages that are then folded and stitched or stapled together, so the total number of pages in any project you'll be sending to a printer must be divisible by four or eight, including covers and blank pages. It may help to make a physical dummy.

STEP 2
PLAN YOUR CONTENT

Making a dummy gives you a good feel of the reader's experience, which can help you decide what content should go where. Any facing pages should work together, even if they aren't designed as a single spread. Bear in mind that text shouldn't cross the gutter, and – except on the centre spread – any images that extend across the gutter could be misaligned.

STEP 3
CREATE A FLAT PLAN

A flat plan is a visual diagram or map of your completed project with a series of thumbnails for each page in sequence. Mapping your project in this way can help identify any potential problems, such as having too much content. You can easily update the plan by reordering pages or content as the project progresses.

STEP 4
USE YOUR FLAT PLAN

As a snapshot of your whole project or publication at a glance, your flat plan can be helpful in both content planning and project management. Mapping the design and editorial elements on each thumbnail, for example, helps check consistency, balance, flow, and rhythm across the whole project. You can also add "status bars" above each thumbnail to indicate what stage the corresponding spread has reached.

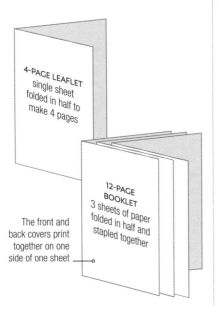

4-PAGE LEAFLET
single sheet folded in half to make 4 pages

12-PAGE BOOKLET
3 sheets of paper folded in half and stapled together

The front and back covers print together on one side of one sheet

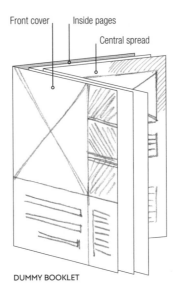

Front cover   Inside pages

Central spread

DUMMY BOOKLET

If you're working on a larger print project, such as a pamphlet, magazine, or book, you'll need to do some initial planning to help organize and visualize its structure, and to ensure you haven't overlooked anything. You may find dummies and flat plans invaluable tools at this stage.

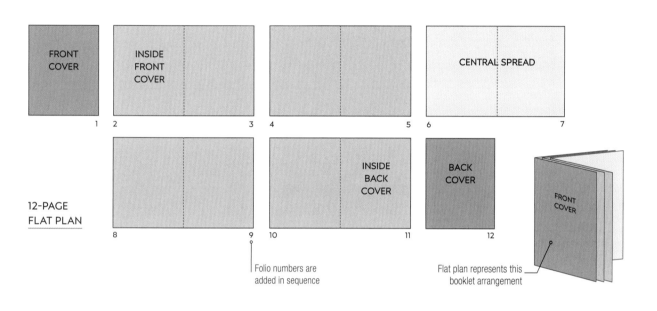

FRONT COVER

INSIDE FRONT COVER

1   2   3   4   5   6   CENTRAL SPREAD   7

12-PAGE FLAT PLAN

8   9   10   INSIDE BACK COVER   11   12   BACK COVER

FRONT COVER

Folio numbers are added in sequence

Flat plan represents this booklet arrangement

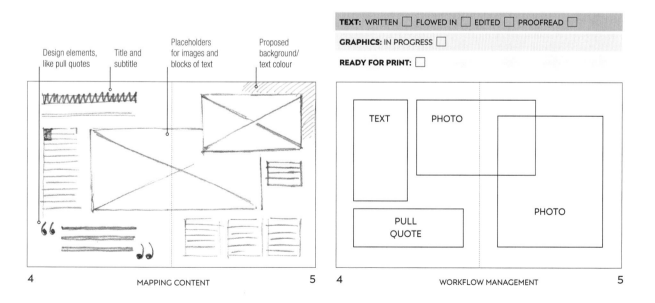

Design elements, like pull quotes

Title and subtitle

Placeholders for images and blocks of text

Proposed background/ text colour

4   MAPPING CONTENT   5

TEXT: WRITTEN ☐ FLOWED IN ☐ EDITED ☐ PROOFREAD ☐

GRAPHICS: IN PROGRESS ☐

READY FOR PRINT: ☐

TEXT   PHOTO

PULL QUOTE

PHOTO

4   WORKFLOW MANAGEMENT   5

PREPARING DESIGNS FOR PRINT

PRINT CHECKLIST

These eight steps will help you to catch any final errors and make sure your project prints as expected.

ASK THE PRINTER

Most printers will help you with any technical aspects of pre-printing that you're not familiar with. Many will be happy to provide specifications and checklists for you to follow – so if you are in any doubt, check with the printer before you prepare your files for printing.

GRAPHIC CHECKS

Look at the overall layout and make sure everything appears as it should. Check that no text is missing, and that features such as size and style of fonts, width of borders, and alignment of elements are consistent. Double-check the document's dimensions to ensure it has been set up at the right size.

PROOFREADING

Proofread all the text. Look for spelling and grammatical errors, and double-check factual information, such as addresses and contact details. Consider asking someone else, preferably not familiar with the project, to do the final proofread – at this stage, you might be too familiar with the text to spot any howlers.

IMAGE RESOLUTION

If your project contains images, check their size and resolution. Raster files such as JPEGs or digital photos should have a resolution of 300dpi or higher, or they may look blurry when printed. Enlarging an image reduces its resolution, so check any enlargements with extra care.

If your design project is going to be professionally printed, you'll need to prepare your files for the printer. Checking your work meticulously at this stage will save you the aggravation – and cost – of putting things right after printing.

COLOUR CHECKS

Your images will need to be saved in CMYK mode (*see* page 74) to be compatible with the printer's four-colour print process. Most digital images are in RGB mode by default (*see* page 74), but you can convert them using design or image-editing software.

BLEED

Make sure your document has been set up with a bleed – an extra area of space that runs beyond the document's edges. Any elements that sit right up against the edge of the page should be extended into the bleed area to give the printer a margin of error when the pages are trimmed to size.

MAKE A PDF

You need to save your design in a set format to send to the printer. This will usually be a PDF, though they may accept other file types, so check first. Most design software will be able to convert your project into a PDF. The process creates a "package" of all the elements in your file so the printer will be able to print your design correctly. You may want to give them a printout for reference, too.

AT THE PRINTER

FINAL CHECK

Always ask the printer for a proof to check before you give the final go-ahead – things can go wrong, even at the printer's end. If you receive the proof digitally, it may help to print it out and look at the hard copy.

PREPARING YOUR WEBSITE FOR LAUNCH

LAUNCH CHECKLIST

Follow these steps to iron out any last issues before you share your website with the world.

BEFORE YOU GO LIVE

CHECK THE CONTENT

Review the site to check that you are using the latest versions of any copy and images, such as logos, contact information, and downloadables. If any content needed client approval, make sure that it's the correct content that is in place, not a draft version.

PROOFREADING

Read all the copy carefully to catch any errors in the spelling, grammar, and punctuation, and don't forget to check headings, buttons, or tags. If possible, ask someone else, who has not worked on the text, to do a final proofread – a fresh pair of eyes may spot errors you have missed.

IMAGE CHECKS

Make sure all the images are optimized so that they look clear and sharp without slowing the site down. Check the file format (photos should be JPEGs; graphics should be PNGs), file size (generally 125–300KB, or up to 1MB for full-screen backgrounds), and resolution (72dpi and above is fine).

LINK TESTING

Click on every link to check that they all work correctly. Do the internal links lead where they are supposed to? Do the external links open the intended content in a new tab? Make sure that any downloadable content downloads quickly and is correct.

Before launching your website, you will need to do a thorough test to check its content and functionality. These final checks are well worth the effort – it will be much trickier and more expensive to correct any glitches once it has gone live.

CONSISTENCY CHECKS

Review the site for uniformity of look and feel. Look out for (unintentionally) jarring spacing, colours, effects, fonts, or images. Make sure the text is styled and formatted consistently across the site, keeping an eye on point size, spacing, and the use of italic, bold, and coloured type.

LEGIBILITY TESTING

Typefaces and point sizes that work well in print may not perform so well online, so check that all the website copy is clearly legible and easy to read. Ideally, get a second opinion from a potential end user. Consider that some people may find smaller or reversed-out type harder to read.

BROWSER AND MOBILE CHECKS

Preview the site on the major web browsers to check it displays and performs correctly, including images and videos. You can use free browser-compatibility testing tools, such as Browsershots. It's also worth checking the site on a variety of devices and platforms. A real-world test is best, but you can preview the site on mobile-emulators such as MobileTest.me, while Google's Mobile-Friendly Test tool gives feedback on mobile compatibility.

LEGAL ISSUES

Make sure you have permission to use any third-party images, fonts, or other content, and that any such content is properly credited. Check that you have included any legally required information, such as a privacy policy, cookie warnings, terms and conditions, and company details. Don't forget to include a copyright line for the site owner.

STREAMLINED SHOWCASE

This understated design shows off the products beautifully, while providing an easy shopping and browsing experience. Viewers find products via the menu bar, the bestsellers panel, or by clicking on images from the social media feed. The different pages have a consistency of design that conveys a cohesive, confident mood.

home   shop   (HC)   about   contact

HOME COMFORTS
BEAUTIFUL THINGS TO STYLE YOUR SPACE

"Simplicity is the ultimate sophistication."

Shop ceramics

Our bestsellers

Details   Add to cart   Details   Add to cart   Details   Add to cart

"Have nothing in your home that you do not know to be useful, or believe to be beautiful."

Check out the latest images on our feed...

♡ 150
How much do I love my new shopping boards? #happycook

(HC)

Contact us   Blog   Instagram   Facebook
Subscribe to our newsletter

HOMEPAGE

DEPARTMENT PAGE

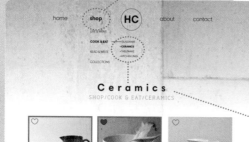

home   shop   (HC)   about   contact

LIVE & WEAR
COOK & EAT   GLASSWARE
                 • CERAMICS
READ & WRITE   • TABLEWARE
                 • KITCHEN LINEN
COLLECTIONS

Ceramics
SHOP/COOK & EAT/CERAMICS

Details   Add to cart   Details   Add to cart   Details   Add to cart

Add to cart

home   shop   (HC)   about   contact

LIVE & WEAR
COOK & EAT   GLASSWARE
                 • CERAMICS
READ & WRITE   • TABLEWARE
                 • KITCHEN LINEN
COLLECTIONS

Ceramics
SHOP/COOK & EAT/CERAMICS

Glazed jugs
From £25

1960s-inspired, ceramic thrown jugs with a high-gloss teal glaze and white accents.

Size
Small   £25
Medium   £35
Large   £45

Quantity
1

Add to cart

Other views   Related objects

PRODUCT PAGE

DESIGN AN **ONLINE SHOP**

E-shoppers want the same as real-world customers – to be able to find the products they want and buy them easily and without fuss. An online shop needs to make the process as seamless and enjoyable as possible.

THE BRIEF

Online shops are mostly set up using an e-commerce platform: whether it's a stand-alone site or a shop facility added to an existing website or blog, these providers handle the technical issues such as hosting and setting up payment systems, leaving you to select a suitable design template and customize it to suit your needs. Here, a small company selling homeware is setting up a shop as part of its website.

JOB SPEC:

- Overall aim: to design a digital shop facility to sit within the company's website.

- Design needs to be consistent with existing assets so as to consolidate the brand, inspire loyalty from existing customers, and attract new business.

- Display products attractively, and provide succinct, informative, and easy-to-access product and price information.

- Provide an easy, transparent payment procedure, to build trust and loyalty.

THE TOOLKIT

This company is already trading, so it has a logo and strapline, plus a set of style guidelines. It also uses a favicon – a small device that acts in place of a logo on websites or social media, where space is tight.

An online shop might require some additional elements, such as an attention-grabbing colour for "Buy" buttons, but the overall design should fit into the existing set of communications materials.

PHOTOS

DESIGN ELEMENTS

Favicon — HC **HOME COMFORTS** BEAUTIFUL THINGS TO STYLE YOUR SPACE — Logo and strapline

COLOUR PALETTE

PALE TEAL
R202 G214 B217

YELLOW
R242 G206 B75

BLACK
R43 G38 B32

TYPEFACES AND FONTS

SOHO PRO THIN

SOHO PRO REGULAR

Harmonia Sans Pro Light

Harmonia Sans Pro Regular

Harmonia Sans Pro Semibold

THE DESIGN PROCESS

WORK OUT THE NAVIGATION

Products must be easy to find and organized in a way that makes sense for the user. Here, items are grouped by what you do with them, then sub-menus appear when you click or hover over a section. Products can appear in more than one sub-menu.

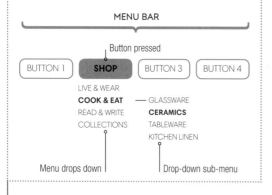

THINK ABOUT PHOTOGRAPHY

An online shop succeeds or fails on the quality of its product images: you could be selling the best products around, but if the photography doesn't do them justice, nobody will buy. Here are some things to think about when shooting products:

- Images should be of the highest quality, to make the experience as close as possible to seeing it in real-life.
- Show an item from different angles, to give the viewer as much information as possible. Consider using a 360-degree photo tool, so items are viewable from every angle.
- Allow viewers to zoom in on images so they can see details.
- Use the same photographic set-up and shooting angle for all images to give a consistent look to your shop page. (This may not be possible if your items are very different sizes.)
- Ensure that your photography styling, colours, and mood reinforce your brand identity.

Shoot products on a plain, white background to convey clear information about them. It's a good idea to include shots of the item in context too, to help the viewer imagine how they might use it themselves.

A useful feature is to make small images clickable to view at a larger size

THINK ABOUT COLOURS

Colour choices should be led by the brand palette. Colours can enliven a design, but take care not to overwhelm the products themselves. Here, the designer opted for mainly white, with teal panels and a banner to help indicate different areas of the shop.

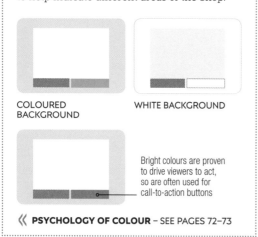

COLOURED BACKGROUND

WHITE BACKGROUND

Bright colours are proven to drive viewers to act, so are often used for call-to-action buttons

« **PSYCHOLOGY OF COLOUR** – SEE PAGES 72–73

Shooting on a white background displays the product with no distraction.

The product in context inspires the viewer and lends a sense of scale.

A tight close-up reveals hidden detail and shows off quality of workmanship.

« **CHOOSE AND USE PHOTO EQUIPMENT** – SEE PAGES 94–95

⟩⟩ ALTERNATIVE DESIGNS

This design uses a modular grid to showcase the products. Using two columns, rather than three, means the images can be bigger. There are no call-to-action buttons to disrupt the sleek layout – viewers click on the images themselves to access more information. Simple yellow bars at the top and bottom frame the content – and the same colour is used for the "Add to basket" button on the pop-up page.

PRODUCT POP-UP

DEPARTMENT PAGE

⌃ SINGLE-PAGE SHOPPING

When clicked, products appear as pop-ups, rather than opening in a new page. This approach can be more user-friendly for shoppers using a hand-held device.

WORKING WITH PROFESSIONALS

COPYWRITER

A skilled wordsmith will help you develop a powerful brand "voice" and write specialist text, such as technical or marketing copy.

PROOFREADER

An experienced proofreader will find and correct errors, and check for consistency to ensure your project has a high-quality, professional finish.

DECIDING WHO YOU NEED

You might be surprised by how many different options you have when it comes to hiring a professional. Being clear on what you need will help you find the right person for the job.

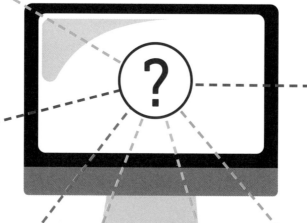

PHOTOGRAPHER

If you need bespoke photographs, consider hiring a photographer. Depending on your project (and budget), you might also need to think about hiring a location and props, as well as a stylist, models, and hair and make-up artists.

IMAGE RESEARCHER

A picture researcher can source hard-to-find images, negotiate fees, and clear rights and permissions.

GRAPHIC DESIGNER

For projects that need advanced graphic-design skills, or if you want to create a strong brand, a trained graphic designer can be a worthwhile investment.

WEB DESIGNER

If you're looking for a complex or unique website, or are developing your own app, it will be well worth engaging the services of an experienced digital designer.

ILLUSTRATOR

Illustrators create original artwork tailored to your needs. Figurative illustrators depict objects, while conceptual illustrators base their work on more abstract ideas.

No matter how talented or enthusiastic you are, sometimes you will need to turn to a professional. Whether it's bespoke artwork, the perfect photograph, or a new app, some specialist skills are best outsourced. Once you've found the right person for the job, it's crucial to give them a clear brief.

FINDING THE RIGHT PERSON

Look through magazines, brochures, and websites you like and keep an eye out for image or writing credits. Word of mouth can also be a good way to find reliable talent: ask friends, colleagues, or even local universities for recommendations.

SEARCHING ONLINE

Make your search terms as specific as possible. Most professionals work within a niche, for example food photographers or technical copywriters, so search using terms that match exactly what you want. To find visual examples, you can also search by image.

AGENCIES

Many illustrators and photographers work with agencies, so agency websites can be a good place to browse portfolios. The quality of work is likely to be high, but agents often charge commission so this route may end up costing you more. Some agencies also have strict rules on rights, so be upfront about your terms.

ASSESSING A PORTFOLIO

Even if someone comes highly recommended, you should always look at their portfolio before getting in touch. You can expect good technical skills as standard, but what about the mood of their work? If their portfolio doesn't excite you, don't be afraid to politely decline. Follow your instincts.

BEFORE YOU MAKE A DECISION

You've found someone whose work you like and who wants to take on the work. But before you commit to working together, ask yourself the following questions:

- Do they seem easy to work with?
- How flexible are they?
- How enthusiastic are they?
- Are they committed to your project's success?
- Do they have a proven track record of reliability?
- Can you afford their rates?

BRIEFING EFFECTIVELY

Clear communication is vital to getting what you want at a price you can afford. Be prepared to be flexible and negotiate where necessary. The questions below will help build your brief.

① WHAT DO YOU WANT?

Explain the context and be as specific as possible, giving examples of work you like. For photographers, illustrators, and designers, give visual references for style and mood as well as any technical specifications. Asking to approve samples during a shoot or rough sketches or designs can save time later. Make any feedback as constructive and specific as you can.

② WHAT IS IT FOR?

If appropriate, specify how many times you'll use the work, at what size, and whether online or in print (if the latter, how many copies will be printed and where will it be published?). For a website, explain exactly what you need it for: does it need to showcase your work? Will it have an online shop?

③ WHEN DO YOU WANT IT BY?

Be clear on your timescale, agree a schedule, and build in extra time for revisions and delays. Be prepared to be flexible on your start time: good creatives often have full calendars.

④ WHAT WILL THE FEE BE?

Professionals usually have standard day or project rates, but you can use your budget as a starting point if you need to negotiate. Be clear on what's included in the fee. For photographers, for example, can they use their own studio or will you need to pay for a location? Do they need an assistant?

⑤ WHAT ARE THE TERMS AND CONDITIONS?

Always put the agreed terms in writing and ask the professional to confirm their acceptance; even a simple email can act as a basic contract. Remember to ask how the work should be credited and who will retain copyright (*see* page 211 for more on legal issues).

PAPER WEIGHTS AND FINISHES

WEIGHTS

The weight of the paper determines how thick it is and how substantial it feels. Heavier weights make a better first impression, convey higher quality, and are more opaque, minimizing show-through on double-sided printing – but they will inevitably incur higher printing and delivery costs.

PAPER WEIGHT TABLE

Paper weight is measured in GSM (grams per square metre) – the higher the GSM, the heavier the paper.

80–100	Basic office paper weight; not suitable for printing
110–120	Stationery paper weight; fine for compliments slips and letterheads
130–170	A more substantial weight; suitable for leaflets, mailshots, posters, and the inside pages of brochures and magazines
170–200	Weighty paper; ideal for brochure or magazine covers and double-sided leaflets
200–250	Card weight; use for brochure or magazine covers if you want a higher-quality finish
300–400	Board weight; perfect for business cards
400+	Heavy board weight; consider using for top-quality business cards

FINISHES

Paper can be either uncoated, meaning the ink soaks into the paper, or coated, meaning the ink sits on top of the surface. The finish you choose can have a big impact on your design.

UNCOATED OR COATED?

	Uncoated	Coated
Look and feel	Traditional, textured, warm, authentic, elegant	Contemporary, smooth, slick, professional, uniform
Colours	Darker and more muted	Brighter and more vibrant
Images	Softer	Sharper
Finishes	Smooth, textured (laid or linen)	Matt, silk/satin, gloss
Good for	Tactile, vintage designs; text-heavy designs (reduces glare)	Sleek, modern designs; photography-heavy designs

COLOURS

The same CMYK colours can look very different in print depending on the colour of the paper stock, as shown right. Most printing is done on white as this is a more neutral base, but even white ranges from warm to cool. You will need to take this into account in your design.

The warmer tones of paper show through the magenta and blue, giving them a weaker, more yellowed appearance.

If you are planning to print your design, you will need to decide what paper stock to use. The paper weight and finish you choose will communicate a message about the quality of your brand or product, so consider your options – and budget – carefully.

SAMPLES

Most printers offer free sample packs of paper stock and printed materials to help you compare weights and printing options. With physical samples, you can check the feel, quality, and opacity of the stock, see the difference between finishes, and get client approval if necessary.

PAPER SAMPLES

SPECIAL INKS

A standard print job is limited to combinations of the four CMYK inks (*see* page 74), so cannot achieve the full spectrum of colour. One way to add impact and make your printed design "pop" is to add a fifth colour by using a special ink. Options include brighter, purer versions of CMYK equivalents (such as bright green), as well as metallics and fluorescents.

SPECIAL PRINT FINISHES

Used effectively, special finishes can make your designs look and feel more professional and impactful. Many printers offer a wide range of special finishes, such as those shown here, though they will usually come at an extra cost. They may also take longer to produce than standard finishes.

Embossing The surface of the paper is raised so that the image stands proud.

Debossing A design is pressed into the paper, creating an indented pattern.

Lasercutting/die-cutting A bespoke shape is cut out of the paper stock.

Foil stamping/blocking Smooth, reflective metallic foil is applied to the surface.

Spot/UV gloss A specific area is accented with a high-gloss coating.

RESOURCES

ISO SERIES

ISO "A" SERIES

Measured in millimetres, the ISO's "A" series is very widely used around the world for items such as business stationery, labels, booklets, notepads, and posters. Sizes in the "A" series officially start at A0, shown as the whole rectangle below. Each size down is half the size of the last.

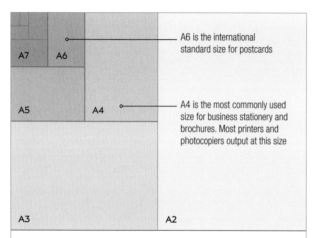

A6 is the international standard size for postcards

A4 is the most commonly used size for business stationery and brochures. Most printers and photocopiers output at this size

FORMAT	WIDTH × HEIGHT
A0	841 × 1189mm
A1	594 × 841mm
A2	420 × 594mm
A3	297 × 420mm
A4	210 × 297mm
A5	148 × 210mm
A6	105 × 148mm
A7	74 × 105mm

A0 is the largest size, taking up the whole area of this diagram

ISO "C" SERIES AND "DL"

The "C" series is mostly used for envelopes. Here, you can see the most popular sizes along with an illustration of how a standard A4 sheet of paper fits inside. The "DL" format is very common for business letters and fits an A4 sheet folded into thirds.

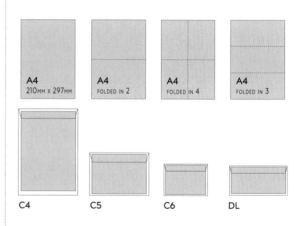

SIZE	WIDTH × HEIGHT
C4	229 × 324mm
C5	162 × 229mm
C6	114 × 162mm
DL	220 × 110mm

Whatever you design, if it's being printed, you need to consider paper size. In North America, standard sizes are set by the ANSI (American National Standards Institute), while almost everywhere else follows the ISO (International Organization for Standardization).

US STANDARD PAPER SIZES

US PAPER SIZES

North American paper sizes are measured in inches. The ANSI B size is commonly known as tabloid when it is in a portrait (vertical) format, and ledger when it is landscape (horizontal). Unlike ISO, ANSI standard sizes do not have a single aspect ratio, so can't be resized as easily.

US ENVELOPE SIZES

There is a wider range of standard envelope sizes in the US, categorized as commercial, announcement, and catalog envelopes. Here we show the commercial sizes. The most popular is the no. 10 as it holds letter paper folded in three, or legal paper folded in four.

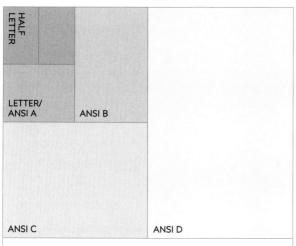

Legal is the same width as letter, but is longer

FORMAT	WIDTH × HEIGHT
Half letter	5.5 × 8.5in
Letter/ANSI A	8.5 × 11in
Legal	8.5 × 14in
ANSI B	11 × 17in
ANSI C	17 × 22in
ANSI D	22 × 34in
ANSI E	34 × 44in

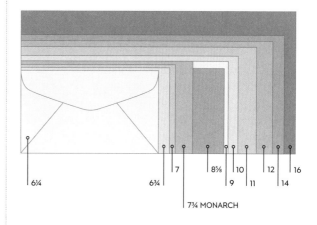

SIZE	WIDTH × HEIGHT	SIZE	WIDTH × HEIGHT
6¼	6 × 3.5in	10	9.5 × 4.125in
6¾	6.5 × 3.625in	11	10.375 × 4.5in
7	6.75 × 3.75in	12	11 × 4.75in
7¾	7.5 × 3.875in	14	11.5 × 5in
8⅝	8.625 × 3.625in	16	12 × 6in
9	8.875 × 3.875in		

LETTER FOLDED IN 3   NO. 10

FINDING DESIGN RESOURCES

WHERE TO FIND FREE DESIGN TOOLS

If you know where to look, you can find lots of free resources for your graphic-design projects, including fonts, apps, images, and software. Cheap paid-for alternatives are another cost-effective option.

 ### FONTS
Your computer and graphic-design or word-processing software come with a set of free fonts, but there are thousands of open-source fonts available online. Simply searching "free fonts" can be overwhelming and may bring up unreliable sources, making it difficult to find the best typeface for the job. Instead, choose trusted sites that curate and classify fonts for you. Searching for the "best sites for free commercial-use fonts" will bring up the latest recommendations, or start with well-known sites such as:

» **Google Fonts**
» **FontSpace**
» **Open Font Library**
» **Open Foundry**
» **Behance**

 ### IMAGES
Sign up to a royalty-free image site (Shutterstock and Getty Images are among the largest) to get access to millions of images, including both photographs and illustrations, for a monthly or annual subscription fee. The images are well classified and easily searchable, so if you're going to be using lots of images in your design projects, it is well worth the cost. You can also find images for free from the sites below.

» **Wikimedia Commons** and **Flickr Creative Commons** host millions of free-to-use public domain or CC0 images (see right).
» **Unsplash** is a collection of free photographs that can be used without a licence (though it's good practice to include a credit).

 ### SOFTWARE
If you already have subscription-based software, such as Adobe Creative Cloud, there are many free "add-on" tools available to download. A search for "Photoshop brushes", for instance, brings up a huge range of open-source digital artwork tools. But if you're not ready to invest in a software subscription, there are many free substitutes. Search for "reviews of free design software", or try options such as the below.

» **GIMP** and **PhotoScape** are free photo-editing software options.
» **Scribus** is a desktop tool for designing page layouts.
» **Inkscape** enables you to create vector artworks.
» **Easel.ly** offers a free version of its infographic-creation software.

Open-source material – such as fonts, images, apps, and software – has built-in permission to be used without charge, and is freely available online. Just be sure you're aware of the potential pitfalls and the basic rules of copyright.

APPS

There are many downloadable apps available to make design tasks easier, quicker, and – in some cases – mobile. Most offer free basic versions as standard but with in-app purchase options.

» **Pantone Studio** identifies colours in photographs and helps you build beautiful colour palettes. Another free palette option is **Coolors**.
» **WhatTheFont** helps you to identify fonts you like from images uploaded to the app.
» **Color Mate** is a cheap app that helps you convert colours between formats, as well as many other features. A search for "colour converters" will bring up free versions.
» **Font Candy** and **Path On** enable you to add text to images using a selection of artistic fonts.
» **Genius Scan** and **Scanbot** (or cheap paid-for options, such as **Scanner Pro**) use smartphone or tablet cameras to generate digital versions of physical documents.

POTENTIAL PITFALLS

If open-source materials are so widely available, why pay for design tools at all? Though generally safe to download and use, there are some drawbacks to using free materials.

» **Limited support**: open-source software is often built by a community of developers, so it's difficult to get technical help.
» **Complex interface**: free software can be more challenging to use as it isn't necessarily developed with the end-user in mind.
» **Viruses and malware**: if you're not discerning about where you source materials, you could inadvertently download a virus. Malevolent users are also able to exploit any vulnerabilities in open-source software.
» **Hidden costs**: some apps that advertise themselves as free can then demand payment to unlock key features. Check reviews before you download.

LEGAL AND COPYRIGHT ISSUES

Every designer needs to have a basic understanding of the copyright law applicable in their country – both in terms of using others' creative work and protecting their own. Fortunately, the guidelines are fairly straightforward.

COPYRIGHT

In law, creative works belong to whoever created or commissioned them – that is, they own the copyright. But if the works were created before copyright existed, if the copyright has expired (in the UK it's 70 years after the creator's death), or if the owner has waived their copyright, the works are free to use.

IMAGE COPYRIGHT

If you've found an image you want to use, you should assume it's in copyright unless it's specified as open source or is in the public domain. It's the designer's responsibility to clear copyright, so be sure to get the right licence. There is usually a fee, and the owner may ask you to include a credit or copyright line. If it's a photograph, you may also need to get permission from anyone in it.

COPYRIGHTING YOUR DESIGNS

Any designs you create as an individual are your intellectual property and you automatically own the copyright – unless you give the rights to whoever commissioned it. You need to apply for trademark protection for logos, though.

FONT LICENSING

Although you're licensed to use the fonts that come with graphic design software, you don't own them, so you can't share them with unlicensed users.

CREATIVE COMMONS LICENCES

These essentially allow you to use, modify, or share the licensed content, though permissions vary. Look for CC0 or "CC BY" (attribution) content which is free to use though may need a credit. See creativecommons.org for details.

COLOUR PALETTE PICKER

AUTUMN

C27 M84 Y66 K25
R128 G72 B71

C14 M84 Y79 K3
R174 G82 B73

C8 M74 Y42 K1
R193 G103 B115

C20 M30 Y100 K0
R192 G164 B62

WOODLAND

C42 M12 Y65 K1
R162 G179 B117

C41 M43 Y42 K27
R122 G113 B108

C21 M61 Y60 K10
R162 G112 B96

C6 M37 Y71 K0
R215 G163 B97

ANTIQUE

C13 M60 Y63 K10
R174 G114 B93

C49 M91 Y22 K10
R122 G74 B113

C88 M55 Y23 K7
R75 G105 B141

C100 M77 Y10 K45
R47 G59 B95

SYNTHETIC

C0 M77 Y0 K0
R209 G102 B157

C5 M0 Y100 K0
R243 G230 B43

C22 M0 Y100 K0
R207 G212 B59

C63 M0 Y100 K0
R126 G174 B80

BEACH

C0 M6 Y80 K0
R250 G225 B84

C0 M13 Y55 K0
R245 G216 B133

C67 M0 Y36 K0
R120 G181 B171

C2 M47 Y100 K0
R214 G144 B57

SUMMER

C51 M0 Y30 K0
R151 G197 B184

C60 M20 Y0 K0
R128 G167 B215

C0 M62 Y66 K0
R212 G122 B94

C0 M90 Y100 K0
R199 G72 B59

50S RETRO

C4 M63 Y76 K1
R201 G117 B82

C40 M16 Y35 K1
R165 G181 B163

C53 M21 Y20 K3
R139 G164 B179

C6 M5 Y67 K0
R238 G224 B113

60S RETRO

C62 M18 Y52 K2
R123 G157 B133

C43 M25 Y58 K8
R146 G152 B116

C95 M60 Y29 K14
R63 G93 B124

C8 M20 Y34 K1
R223 G199 B165

70S RETRO

C45 M61 Y84 K63
R69 G60 B41

C22 M39 Y94 K12
R164 G135 B65

C51 M40 Y80 K31
R103 G104 B71

C14 M68 Y61 K3
R181 G108 B96

If you're looking for inspiration for your next project, here is a selection of colour palettes, complete with colour values for print or digital use, that you can be confident will work well. Use them as they are, or as a starting point for your own creative combinations.

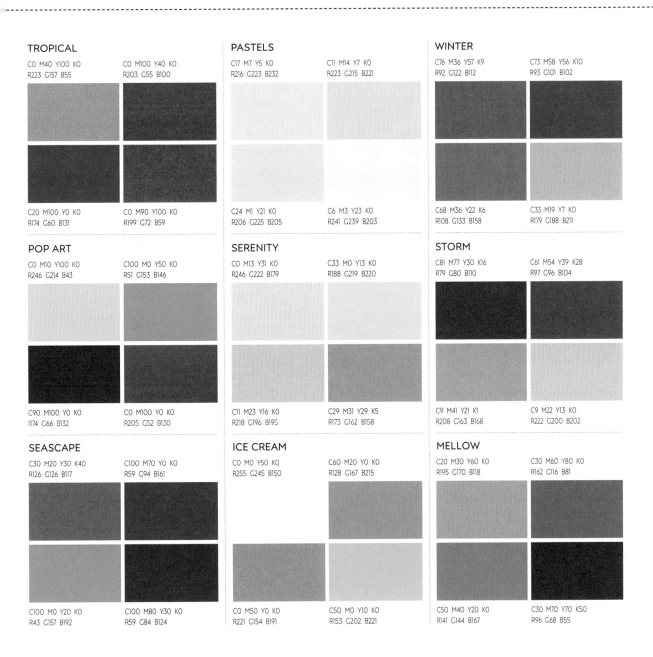

TROPICAL

C0 M40 Y100 K0
R223 G157 B55

C0 M100 Y40 K0
R203 G55 B100

C20 M100 Y0 K0
R174 G60 B131

C0 M90 Y100 K0
R199 G72 B59

PASTELS

C17 M7 Y5 K0
R216 G223 B232

C11 M14 Y7 K0
R223 G215 B221

C24 M1 Y21 K0
R206 G225 B205

C6 M3 Y23 K0
R241 G239 B203

WINTER

C76 M36 Y57 K9
R92 G122 B112

C73 M58 Y56 K10
R93 G101 B102

C68 M36 Y22 K6
R108 G133 B158

C33 M19 Y7 K0
R179 G188 B211

POP ART

C0 M10 Y100 K0
R246 G214 B43

C100 M0 Y50 K0
R51 G153 B146

C90 M100 Y0 K0
R74 G66 B132

C0 M100 Y0 K0
R205 G52 B130

SERENITY

C0 M13 Y31 K0
R246 G222 B179

C33 M0 Y13 K0
R188 G219 B220

C11 M23 Y16 K0
R218 G196 B195

C29 M31 Y29 K5
R173 G162 B158

STORM

C81 M77 Y30 K16
R79 G80 B110

C61 M54 Y39 K28
R97 G96 B104

C9 M41 Y21 K1
R208 G163 B168

C9 M22 Y13 K0
R222 G200 B202

SEASCAPE

C30 M20 Y30 K40
R126 G126 B117

C100 M70 Y0 K0
R59 G94 B161

C100 M0 Y20 K0
R43 G157 B192

C100 M80 Y30 K0
R59 G84 B124

ICE CREAM

C0 M0 Y50 K0
R255 G245 B150

C60 M20 Y0 K0
R128 G167 B215

C0 M50 Y0 K0
R221 G154 B191

C50 M0 Y10 K0
R153 G202 B221

MELLOW

C20 M30 Y60 K0
R195 G170 B118

C30 M60 Y80 K0
R162 G116 B81

C50 M40 Y20 K0
R141 G144 B167

C30 M70 Y70 K50
R96 G68 B55

GLOSSARY

Additive mixing Creating colours for digital screens by mixing varying amounts of red, green, and blue light.

Alignment The lining up of text or design objects along a line or margin, in order to organize information visually. Items can be aligned to the left, to the right, or centrally.

Ascender The part of a lowercase letter that extends above the x-height.

Audit In marketing, an analysis of aspects of an organization or company's style and performance. Audits can be undertaken of one's own business or those of peers and competitors.

Balance Describes how design elements are combined in order to achieve a sense of visual equilibrium on the layout.

Baseline In typography, an invisible line on which lowercase letters sit.

Baseline grid A series of horizontal lines on a layout grid, upon which lines of text sit.

Bitmap image See Raster image.

Bleed Describes content that extends outside the bounds of a print layout so that when the page is trimmed, the content runs to the edge of the page.

Brand The overall identity of a business, product, or service as others experience it. Every brand has verbal, visual and emotional components.

Brand story A cohesive narrative of all aspects of a brand, designed to help an audience identify better with it.

Brand plan A schedule for a brand's development, up to its launch and beyond. It can be used to track the project's progress.

Cap-height The height of a font's uppercase letters. Also, an invisible line along the top of those letters.

Character In typography, any single letter, numeral, or punctuation mark within a font.

CMYK Stands for cyan, magenta, yellow, and black (the "k" actually stands for "key") – the colours used in the four-colour printing process.

Colour mode A description, in numerical values, of how a colour can be recreated in different media. Colour modes include RGB, CMYK, and HEX.

Colour palette A combination of colours selected for a design project.

Colour picker Computer tool that saves a colour, analyses it and records its digital make-up.

Colour wheel A circular representation of the spectrum that shows how colours contrast and harmonize.

Column A vertical block of text.

Composition The conscious arrangement of selected design elements to create a coherent layout.

Cropping Cutting away unwanted parts of an image.

Cutout An image with its background removed by a photo-editing tool.

Dead space An empty area within a design space that has no positive effect on a composition.

Desaturation Describes the reduction or removal of colour from an image.

Descender The part of a lowercase letter that extends below the baseline.

Digitizing Turning a non-digital image such as a pencil drawing into a digital file by means of scanning or photography.

Display typeface One that has been designed specifically for use at large sizes in headings. Display typefaces are also often extravagantly styled.

DPI (Dots per inch) Method used to describe the resolution of a digital image. The higher the DPI, the more dots (or pixels) it contains, and the more detail the image will have.

Favicon Short for "favourite icon", this describes a small image, specifially designed for small screens, that identifies a brand.

File format Describes different methods of digitally encoding, storing and transferring data. Common file formats include PDF and JPEG.

Flat plan A sequential diagram of a printed project, with each spread shown as a thumbnail image.

Font A sub-group of a typeface, in which all the characters have the same specific style – for instance, bold or italic. The term is often inaccurately used interchangeably with "typeface".

Format The size, shape, and medium in which a design is produced.

Glyphs Special, non-Roman characters in a font, such as © for copyright. Some glyphs are intended to be purely decorative.

Golden ratio In layout design, a pleasing proportion, based on a mathematical formula, in which elements can be sized and positioned. It gives rise to the golden spiral, an effective tool for cropping images.

Graphic design The arrangement of type and image for the purpose of visual communication.

Grid A structure that sits invisibly beneath a layout and helps the designer to position elements. A grid usually consists of multiple columns and modules.

Grouping Visually linking related design elements by various means, including enclosing them, positioning them in certain ways, or styling them in a similar way.

Gutter The gap between columns or blocks of text, or between the two facing pages that make up a spread.

Hamburger An icon, made up of three horizontal lines, which indicates an on-screen menu.

Hierarchy The relative importance of elements within a layout.

Horizontal format Describes an image, page, or screen format that is wider than it is tall. Also described as landscape format.

Hue A named colour, taken from the main colours of the spectrum.

Image editing Changing an image digitally by adjusting its contrast, colour, brightness, and so on.

Italics (oblique) A font style designed to slope to the right.

Justified Describes text that aligns in a straight line along both the left- and right-hand sides.

Kerning Adjusting the space between two individual characters.

Landscape format See Horizontal format.

Layout The arrangement of all the visual elements within a defined design space, such as a page.

Leading The horizontal space between lines of text, measured in points.

Legibility A measure of how easy it is to read text within a layout. Factors that affect legibility include height and colour of type, and size of leading.

Ligature A single new character created by joining two or more characters, such as "f" and "i".

Logo A visual representation of an organization or product. A logo can be text-only, an image or symbol, or a combination of both.

Macro space Gaps between larger elements in a design, such as images and columns of text.

Margin The area between the main content and the top, bottom, left, and right edges of the layout.

Market map A visual study of a market sector, which enables a business to identify trends in its sector, or find gaps in the market.

Measure Describes the length of a line of text; usually expressed in millimetres, inches, or points.

Medium
a) In art, a means of expression such as watercolour or pastels.
b) In technology, a means of communicating a design – print, smartphone, and so on.

Micro space Describes the small spaces between letters and words.

Mind map A branching diagram of a project or concept, visualizing qualities such as aims, values, personality, and target customers. Also known as a spider digram.

"Mobile first" design Design that is created initially for the smartphone, then amended as necessary to suit other media.

Modular design Dividing a layout area into multiple identical blocks of space, known as modules.

Moodboard A collection of images and objects used to inspire creativity. It can be an actual board or created digitally.

Orientation In web design, describes the way in a which a screen is being viewed – either horizontally or vertically.

PDF A versatile file format that is designed to be readable across many different devices and platforms. The most popular and reliable format for sending files to a printer.

Point In typography, points are used to measure type and leading. There are 72 points to one inch.

Portrait format See Vertical format.

Point size Describes the relative height of fonts.

Primary research Research conducted directly with potential customers in interviews, focus groups, and surveys.

Pull-out quote A section copied from the text and repeated at a larger size for emphasis, or to draw the eye to relevance.

Raster image A complex digital image, formed by dots of colour (pixels). Its file formats include JPEG, TIFF, PNG, and PSD. Also known as a bitmap image.

Resolution In a bitmap image, describes the number of coloured dots (pixels) per inch). The lower the resolution, the less detailed an image will be.

Responsive design A system of web-page creation that is able to detect a viewer's screen size and orientation automatically, then rearrange the layout accordingly.

Reversed out Describes light-coloured text that sits on a darker background.

RGB Stands for red, green, blue – the three colours that are mixed to create all the colours on a digital screen.

Roman Describes the standard font in a typeface, with upright characters, as opposed to italics.

Rule of thirds The division of a design space or image into a grid of nine equal-sized areas. Crucial design elements are placed where the lines intersect (know, as sweet spots).

Sans serif Describes typefaces without serifs, such as Helvetica.

Scale In design, the size of an element or group of elements in relation to others within the layout.

Script typeface A typeface modelled on the strokes created by handwriting.

Secondary research Examining and analysing data already collected by others – for example, reports, studies, or newspaper articles.

Serif A small, decorative stroke at the end of a main stroke of a letterform. Also describes a typeface that uses serifs, such as Palatino.

Shade A darker version of a hue.

Spider diagram see Mind map.

Spot colour A colour that is printed using one specific ink, rather than by the four-colour process.

Stock In printing, a specific type of paper, with a certain weight, coating and texture.

Stock image A pre-existing image that can be sourced and used, either free of charge or for an agreed fee.

Strapline A line of text often used to accompany a logo or under a main heading.

Stroke Any of the single parts that make up a letterform.

Subtractive mixing Creating colours for printing by mixing dyes of cyan, magenta, yellow, and black.

Tint A lighter version of a hue.

Tone/tonal value The overall qualities of a hue, including evenness, brightness, and depth.

Tone of voice How an organization or business 'speaks' to its audience – its communication style.

Tracking Also known as letter-spacing, the equal adjustment of spacing between all the characters in a selected piece of text.

Type The symbols we use to convey language and meaning – most importantly, letters and numbers.

Typeface A family of type that shares a common design across its different styles and weights.

Typography The planned and creative use of type to convey a specific meaning.

Vector image A clean, crisp digital image, formed of connected lines called paths.

Vertical format Describes an image, page, or screen format taller than it is wide. Also known as portrait format.

Vibration A "glowing" effect created when two complementary colours of similar tone are placed together.

Visual weight Describes how much a design element attracts attention. It is determined by factors such as size, colour, tone, and texture.

Website template Software that provides a ready-made structure to design and generate web pages.

Weight The thickness of the strokes in a typeface. Weight can range from extra-light to ultra-black.

Wireframe A simple plan of a website, showing where content will be placed and how pages are connected. Wireframes can be hand-drawn or digital.

White space Blank areas (not necessarily white) that make a positive contribution to the look and effectiveness of a design.

x-height The height of the lowercase "x" in a typeface.

INDEX

ACKNOWLEDGMENTS

FROM CATH CALDWELL

Writing this book was a pleasure. But my aim to simplify the field of graphic design was tricky, because it is constantly expanding with new software and terminology emerging almost faster than we could write. For all we know, "favicon" could be ancient history before you know it.

To help me help you, I called on my trusted friends who teach both beginners and experts. I want to give special thanks to authors Emily Wood and Julia Woollams, who I dragged away from their studios and students and to Jamie Hearn who is busy with his own design work and also teaching at my beloved Central Saint Martins. Throughout all this, the fourth writer Johnny Belknap cast his expert typographer's eye over the pages. Johnny is my partner in business and in life and made many pots of tea when I was working on this early in the morning before going to my regular job. I also relied on my family and friends for this team effort. You know who you are.

Thanks go to Karen Sims, Tim Leahy, Sam, Ed, and Daisy Belknap and Anna McCalll who gave me ideas for this ever-changing subject. Thanks also to my students who both inspire me and keep me up to date.

The miracle workers at DK are second to none. The determined Rona Skene is fiercely dedicated to clarity and humanity in this book and prepared to go the extra mile to get there. Graphic designer Alison Gardner is a magician of design and developed all these layouts to help you understand the content. A big thanks goes to Dawn Henderson who had faith in me when she commissioned the book. In true DK tradition, I am proud that she and Rona also wanted the book to speak to everyone interested in the skills of graphic design. I hope you enjoy it.

FROM THE PUBLISHER

We would like to thank the following for their help in the production of this book: Alastair Laing for editorial expertise; Glenda Fisher, Clare Joyce, and Karen Constanti for design assistance; Steve Hill and Angela Martin for expert technical and professional advice; Kirsti Brown (kirstibrownceramics.co.uk), Clare Mackie (claremackie.co.uk), Karen ... (knowandlove.co.uk), Lindsay Skene ... tree-flowers.co.uk), and Kathryn ... (www.kathrynwilliamson.com) ... permission to reproduce ... work; Marie Lorimer for ... hn Friend for proofreading.

PICTURE CREDITS

The publisher would like to thank the following for their kind permission to reproduce their photographs:

(Key: a-above; b-below/bottom; c-centre; f-far; l-left; r-right; t-top):

35 Dreamstime.com: Penchan Pumila / Gamjai (cr/Sack); Sergiy Bykhunenko / Sbworld4 (cr/Wood). 42 Alamy Stock Photo: ACORN 1 / Apple and the Apple logo are trademarks of Apple Inc. (clb); AztecBlue (c); Sergio Azenha (cr); Grzegorz Knec / The NIKE name and the Swoosh design are trademarks of NIKE Inc. (crb). Twitter: TWITTER and the Twitter logo are trademarks of Twitter, Inc. or its affiliates (cb). 43 Alamy Stock Photo: Avangard Photography / Instagram's trademarks, including Instagram, and the Instagram logo are all owned by Instagram (clb); Andrei Stanescu (cl); Frédéric Vielcanet (c); Takatoshi Kurikawa (cr). Chanel: CHANEL is a trademark of CHANEL, INC. (cb). Thai Airways: The THAI's or partners' trademarks, trade names, service marks, logos and all related products or service names, design marks, or slogans are the properties of THAI and of its partners (cr). 44 Alamy Stock Photo: Hemis (cl); Kim Kaminski (c); Peter Probst / FERRARI is a trademark of Ferrari S.p.A. (clb). PENGUIN and the Penguin logo are trademarks of Penguin Books Ltd: (crb). World Wildlife Fund: © 2019 WWF - World Wide Fund For Nature © 1986 Panda Symbol WWF – World Wide Fund For Nature (formerly World Wildlife Fund) ® "WWF" is a WWF Registered Trademark (cb). 45 Alamy Stock Photo: Cal Sport Media (cl); Danny Nebraska (cr); Grzegorz Knec / The intellectual property rights are the sole property of Inter IKEA Systems B.V. (clb). Dreamstime.com: Alexandr Blinov (cl). FedEx: FEDEX is a trademark of Federal Express Corporation (cb). illy: ILLY® and illy logo are registered trademarks of illycaffè S.p.A. via Flavia 110 - 34147 Trieste — Italy. © 2019 illy caffè North America, Inc. All rights reserved (crb). 79 123RF.com: Mark Grenier / nemosdad (cb). Dreamstime.com: (crb). 84 Dreamstime.com: John braid / Johnbraid (cr). 85 123RF.com: Hans Christiansson (cla). Dreamstime.com: Radomír Režný (cb). 86 Bridgeman Images: Private Collection / DaTo Images (cra). Getty Images: Found Image Holdings Inc / Corbis Historical (crb). Photo Scala, Florence: Digital image, The Museum of Modern Art, New York (cl). 87 Bridgeman Images: Private Collection / DaTo Images (cr). Internationale Filmfestspiele Berlin: © Internationale Filmfestspiele / Velvet Creative Office (clb). Photo Scala, Florence: Digital image, The Museum of Modern Art, New York (cla). 88 Alamy Stock Photo: AF Fotografie (crb); Universal Art Archive (cl). The Solomon R. Guggenheim Museum, New York: Poster featuring Malcolm Grear Designers ' 1969 graphic of the Frank Lloyd-Wright designed Guggenheim Museum (tr). 89 Alamy Stock Photo: Pictorial Press Ltd (cla). Bridgeman Images: Private Collection / Photo © Christie's Images (cra). Knoll, Inc.: Courtesy Knoll Archive (crb). Photo Scala, Florence: Digital image, The Museum of Modern Art, New York (clb). 93 PunchStock: Digital Vision (cl). 96 Dreamstime.com: Kmiragaya (cl); Leo Bruce Hempell / Leobruce (c); Sic2005 (cr). Jamie Marshall: (bc). 98 Dreamstime.com: Epicstock (cr). 99 Dreamstime.com: Kmiragaya (cr, crb). 100 123RF.com: stillfx (cb). Dorling Kindersley: Stephen Oliver (crb/Used Twice). Kathryn Willamson: kathrynwilliamsonjewellery.com (cra). 101 123RF.com: stillfx (Used five times on the spread). Dorling Kindersley: Norman Taylor / Bolton Library and Museum Services (ca). Kathryn Willamson: kathrynwilliamsonjewellery.com (tl, cra, crb). 102 Dreamstime.com: Louloua Asgaraly / Lulu432 (cr). 102-103 Dreamstime.com: Pavel Losevsky / Paha_l (c). 103 Dreamstime.com: Epstock (cb). 104-105 Dreamstime.com: Ian Woolcock (Used six time s on the spread). 104 Dreamstime.com: Ben Eastwood (Used thrice on page). 107 Dreamstime.com: Ian Woolcock (crb). 119 Dreamstime.com: Karola-eniko Kallai (cl). Clare Mackie: www.claremackie.co.uk (crb). 120 Alamy Stock Photo: EyeBrowz. 121 Alamy Stock Photo: MPVCVRART (crb). Photo Scala, Florence: Digital image, The Museum of Modern Art, New York (clb). 123 Alamy Stock Photo: dcphoto (cla); Granamour Weems Collection (cra); TheCoverVersion (cl); sjvinyl (crb). 131 Dreamstime.com: Craig Hanson / Rssfhs (c). 132 Dreamstime.com: Vladimir Mudrovcic (crb). 148 Daisy Babbington and Tim Jordan: (clb). 149 Dorling Kindersley: Mark Winwood / RHS Chelsea Flower Show 2014 (c). Dreamstime.com: Margojh (crb). Daisy Babbington and Tim Jordan: (cb). 150 Daisy Babbington and Tim Jordan: (cra). 151 Daisy Babbington and Tim Jordan: (crb). 153 Bridgeman Images: Pictures from History (clb). 164-167 Lindsay Skene: www.lindentree-flowers.co.uk / All images. 182 http://multimediaguides.culture.pl: (t). https://voguegirl.jp: (clb). https://www.tate.org.uk: (crb). 183 http://a-g-i.org: (cb). https://www.knowandlove.co.uk/: (tl). https://www.bose.de: (tr). 184 https://pinupmagazine.org/#34: (tl). https://timberlinetours.com: (tr). https://www.croydonist.co.uk/: (cb). 185 http://porschevolution.com: (clb). https://cowboy.com: (t). https://www.nikon.co.jp/technology/: (crb). 192 Dreamstime.com: Vladimir Mudrovcic (clb/used twice). 200-203 Karen Sims: www.knowandlove.co.uk / All images. 207 Dreamstime.com: Igor Marusitsenko (bc)

All other images © Dorling Kindersley
For further information see: www.dkimages.com